AN
UNLIKELY
ADVENT

An Unlikely Advent: Extraordinary People of the Christmas Story

An Unlikely Advent
978-1-7910-2897-8
978-1-7910-2896-1 eBook

An Unlikely Advent: DVD
978-1-7910-2900-5

An Unlikely Advent: Leader Guide
978-1-7910-2899-2
978-1-7910-2898-5 eBook

RACHEL BILLUPS

AN
UNLIKELY
ADVENT

EXTRAORDINARY PEOPLE OF
THE CHRISTMAS STORY

Abingdon Press | Nashville

To my mom, Linda Fast

You fanned the flame,
and I am grateful.

CONTENTS

CONTENTS

INTRODUCTION

I watched as Carolyn, a member of the worship design team, gently unwrapped the delicate pieces of our church's beloved antique Nativity set one by one. They were cast in white porcelain, and I had just learned that one of our older church faithfuls had handcrafted each Nativity character and presented the set to the church. Worn by years of handling, certain characters were already chipped and stored out of sight until they could be properly repaired.

Carolyn went on to explain that this Nativity set was special. At first it had been displayed within reach of little ones walking through the preschool hallway, but it did not take long to realize that curious hands find their way to the manger unintentionally further damaging the set. The set had to be moved. So, we moved it together.

"It's a beauty," I said, and I meant it. The Nativity set was gorgeous and pristine. It was beautiful but honestly a little bit unrealistic. The Holy Family huddled together in the dark dampness of a straw-filled cave seemed a far cry from the white porcelain I saw before me now.

Nativity scenes function as the centerpiece of nearly every Christmas gathering in our homes and in our churches. It's a holy spot that we attempt to re-create our interpretations of the Gospel stories. So, we gather wise men, Mary and Joseph, a shepherd, and a camel, just to name a few. And then it hit me, what about everyone else in the Christmas story? Why only include Mary, Joseph, and the baby Jesus? Some Nativities include the frequent extras: a side-angel and a few assorted barnyard animals; but what about Zechariah and Elizabeth there in that inner circle? Where is Herod in the grand scheme of things? How did the magi and the shepherds encounter the Christ child?

These B-players usually emerge as "extras" in God's story, but I could not help but wonder if they might have more to teach us about the intersection of God's story with ours. I realized over those years that I somehow relate more closely to shepherds and magi than to Mary and Joseph. And, I am definitely no angel. Could it be that we more readily see ourselves in these unlikely characters surrounding the Advent story?

> Perhaps you will discover that your unlikely story is more aligned with these men and women than you first realized, and ultimately that their story and yours are part of God's unfolding of the Christmas story.

Perhaps we find ourselves in their imperfections, rendering them more accessible, more real-life than the Holy Family. This Advent, we are going on an unlikely journey, reading the stories of these unlikely characters anew. Maybe you will discover that your unlikely story is more aligned with these men and women than you first realized, and ultimately that their story and yours are part of God's unfolding of the Christmas story.

Working through the weeks of Advent, we will start in the first chapter with dreams, or should I say, broken dreams. Our broken dreams are often born out of what we may affectionately call our glory days. How often do we keep our eyes fixed on the rearview mirror, believing that our best days are behind us? Have you ever watched a dream pass you by and thought to yourself, *I missed it, I've missed my shot?* Zechariah and Elizabeth did. Zechariah and Elizabeth believed that they were past their prime, until one day an angel of the Lord showed up and transformed their perspective. Could it be that Zechariah and Elizabeth give us a future *hope* that we didn't even know we needed? For anyone who has ever felt too old, no longer useful, or past their prime, let God transform your perspective: What If I Missed It?

In chapter 2, I unapologetically want to change your perspective about what Herod has to teach us. Characters of good and evil make for exciting stories, yet left unchecked the villains—even the ones inside our heads—can keep us paralyzed. These perceived limitations threaten to keep us bound, yet God wants to birth something new in each of us. God wants to give us perspective on the Herod within. What if you dared to challenge that inner limitation to step into something new? It's time to overcome those negative narratives and embrace the scandalous *love* of God: Playing the Villain.

The magi in chapter 3 have something to teach us about who we believe deserves a front row seat in the Advent story. So often we expect God to act in certain ways within the prescribed confines of our characters and categories. But what if God wants to move in a different direction and use those outside your prescribed faith circle to empower your way forward? Let's rediscover the *joy* of stargazing—reimagining God's kingdom connections—and how to innovate beyond the perceived boundaries of our faith tradition. Let's extend the edges of God's table and ours: A Curious People.

Our final week we will allow ordinary shepherds to lead the way to the manager. Have you ever had an experience that changed everything, an unlikely God-encounter that interrupted the trajectory of your life? Luke's Christmas story describes shepherds as ordinary folks working the night shift when God shows up and messes with their mundane—inviting them to be part of a story bigger than what they'd ever experienced. Angels announced, "There's a new kind of *peace* in town and discovering it will change everything!" What if God shows up in your unlikely story this holiday season? Advent might just be the best time for a God-encounter: When God Shows Up.

The invitation is open to take this four-week Advent journey together. A journey to explore our longings—our hopes and our fears—alongside the characters that function more like sidekicks than the main attraction. With honesty and vulnerability, we will discover stories of pain and promise, jealousy and joy, as real-life people encountering an incarnational presence. My prayer is ultimately for you to explore your own unlikely story for an unlikely Advent.

Your Unlikely Story

In October of 2021, I left a leadership board meeting in a hurry. I knew I had over two hours of driving ahead of me. I was headed to my childhood home in the heart of the Hocking Hills, Ohio. It would be a very short trip: spend the night, get up, do some work, and attend my uncle's funeral. My uncle had passed away after a battle with cancer, and my cousins are just too important to me to miss such a moment in their lives. Therefore, I did what I set out to do: arrive late at night, catch some sleep, get up early, do some church work, and have a little breakfast with my mom and dad. I was so efficient with my time that I was able to take a walk with my mom around the farm.

It was a glorious morning! The air was crisp, the leaves were vibrant yellows and oranges with a few reds speckled in between. Stepping into the cool air, my heart swelled with joy. My mom and I walked the entire perimeter of their hundred-acre farm. The cattle were giving us skeptical looks as we talked about all the fall has to offer.

The time flew by and before we knew it was time to get dressed and go to the funeral. I dressed: black outfit, pearls, and heels—you know, funeral ready. My parents drove separately to pick up my grandma, so rather than follow my parents, I decided to drive an alternative route: Thompson Ridge Road.

The road is full of twists and turns. It's an incredible road to drive as the leaves are transforming in the fall. I knew the road well, so I also knew I could pick up the pace. I was excited, I was ready to enjoy the drive as much as I had enjoyed the morning. And then the moment I made a left turn onto Thompson Ridge Road, I noticed a car in the ditch and someone in it. Everything inside of me said, "Rachel you have to stop!"

I quickly pulled over and jumped out, my high heels clicking on the pavement. I tapped on the window, "You okay in there?" The middle-aged woman looked at me with distress in her eyes as she cracked the window open.

"Yeah," she remarked, "but I can't get my car out. I was just trying to look at my GPS and I slid off the side of the road." I could totally see why! Without enough shoulder space, the leaves and mud made the slide into the ditch a sure thing.

"Let me see if I can help," I heard myself say, "I'll grab some shoes."

I had running shoes in the car so I quickly changed shoes and attempted to push her out, praying I would not get covered in mud in the process. The tires just kept spinning. The woman was desperate: "I can't afford a tow, I'm out here cleaning cabins."

"Okay," I said, "Let me make a few phone calls."

A plan was emerging in my head to ask my great uncle from the other side of my family to help me out. He was cutting wood on our farm. So, I asked if he could come and pull her car out with his truck. I asked for her name.

"Sharon, I am going to give you my cell phone number," I said to her. "I will tell you who is coming to help so you are not surprised, but I must go to this funeral. Oh, and Sharon, you should know I was not supposed to be on this road. I believe that God sent me to you. That is how mindful the God of the universe is of you. God really does love you!"

We hugged and I drove to the funeral, still worrying about Sharon. In that moment I questioned, "God, why was I unable to push her out?" I wanted to be a blessing and instead I drove to the funeral with Sharon and her situation heavy on my mind. I was so worried. But then about twenty minutes later I received a text: "Your uncle came! I'm out! Thank you! You have no idea how much you helped me today. May God be with you all as you bury your loved one."

I was not the hero that day; God was the hero! This unlikely encounter reminded me that life is not all about me. Life is about all of us: you, me, and everybody else! We are so divinely interconnected that God works through our lives to bring help, hope, and healing to the people around us. And particularly in this Advent season, I cannot help but especially remind those of you who have experienced great loss that God is mindful of you. Immanuel, God is with us!

I do not pretend to understand it all. But I know God is continuously weaving together God's purpose and plan through your life into mine and vice versa. Even the simplest experiences and challenges matter to God as God weaves together this unlikely story. It will be incredible! But let's not confuse life as a tranquil, quiet walk in the park because as you and I know, the journey can be more than a little rocky.

Perhaps that is your story? Life has been a little bit rocky, and your faith has been a long process. Faith is a muscle that you have developed over the years. At first, it was hard to say yes to God, even downright scary. But after a few years of building trust, your faith muscle is stronger. When you feel the nudge of God you say yes more quickly. You have spiritual muscle memory. Your faith is stronger, and you are done trusting your own sense of direction! You have let go of control. You have given God permission to take the reins. You have surrendered your own agenda for God's agenda. Why? Because you no longer worry about the destination or getting there in a hurry. You are trusting God all along the way with an extra pair of shoes in the back seat of your vehicle. You have realized that saying yes to God means God speaks, you listen, somebody else gets blessed.

The Advent season finds us smack dab inside the most wonderful but busy time of the year. It's tough to be fully present, from the Thanksgiving meals gathered around the table straight on through to everything Christmas. But when the Christmas presents are all unwrapped and the parties are over, when that last song has been sung, do we really arrive at the place we were hoping? Or are we merely surviving? What if you were open to God's direction, you were listening, and you said yes to God? Well friend, maybe, just maybe, somebody else gets blessed!

I imagine there are some of you wrestling with your God purpose! You want answers and you want direction, like yesterday! You have said right out loud to God: just make it plain! God, please give me a clear five-year plan! God, I need to know that I'm going to be okay. I need to know I'm living my best life possible.

> **Your God-purpose is going to call you into an openness to what God has for you every single day, one day at a time.**

Here's the challenge: God's only telling you to get up and go day by day by day. There is no five-year plan, there is no total security, there is no "life is going to be easy" or "get ready for comfortable"! When it's God's plan, you've got to trust God to fulfill it. When it's God's purpose for your life, you've got to trust God for courage to pull through. When it's God's plan, it's going to be bigger than you. Your God-purpose is going to call you into an openness to what God has for you every single day, one day at a time. What does God want you to do today? Who are you called to pull out of the mud?

Let's practice saying no to merely surviving. Let's say no to the so-so agenda we plan for ourselves. And let's say yes to this journey of interconnectedness and fulfillment. Let us say yes to actively waiting for what God wants to birth in you and in me and through all of us. Because, like it or not, we are *so* connected.

We Are Connected

Our God-purpose is bound up in every other person on the planet. We have an individual destiny, woven into a communal design! We cannot get away from the fact that we are intrinsically connected in a tangible and meaningful way. We are connected to one another and to this God child who was born two thousand years ago. We are interconnected to God's story! Our lives are not just random. We are not islands. The God at work in the lives of Joseph, Mary, and their Son, our Savior, is the same God at work in our lives to break the cycles of struggle that have us bound up.

> This unlikely Advent story is not about you or me or any one of us being healed in isolation. We are healed in community.

This unlikely Advent story is not about you or me or any one of us being healed in isolation. We are healed in community. We find hope together as we hear children sing songs of the season. We understand the kingdom of God just a bit more when words are set to music, and we soak in the messages of truth and light in new ways. We are connected once again when together we sing familiar words both ancient and future in the hymn "O Come, O Come Emmanuel"!

If there is one thing I have learned in these last pandemic years, it is that healing, the fulfillment of our collective purpose, cannot take place separate from the people around us. It is not just Jesus 'n me. It's Jesus, me, you, and everyone else. And what if we

Introduction

dared to acknowledge this gift of one another and set out to live more connected than we ever imagined?

We cannot do faith alone; we are bound up together, connected as the body of Jesus. I need you and you need me. Are you ready to pour your life into the people around you? Are you ready to throw an extra pair of shoes into your back seat and listen for God to speak? Are your eyes and calendar open for an unlikely encounter? We are not rugged individualists determined to survive. We are interconnected faith followers of Jesus created to thrive, no matter what life brings our way. We are in this together. And I cannot wait to hear how God shapes and reshapes your unlikely story throughout this Advent season.

1

What If I Missed It?

Chapter 1
WHAT IF I MISSED IT?

Growing up, I was obsessed with pictures of Mary and baby Jesus. I collected prints of Renaissance paintings and ancient icons and taped them to the inside of my high school locker. While I was mystically drawn to the Madonna and child, it was a bonus to encounter a portrayal of the entire Holy Family. Typically, in a creche of the Nativity, huddled together in the glow of the straw-filled cave, Mary, Joseph, and baby Jesus seemed pristine, other-worldly. This picturesque scene is and was a popular household display.

Perhaps you felt the same way growing up. There was a bit of awe and wonder when looking at a classic Nativity set. But what about everybody else in the Christmas story? Ever wonder why your standard Nativity sets only include a handful of characters: Mary, Joseph, baby Jesus, an angel, a sheep, maybe a cow or two? What about Uncle Zechariah and Aunt Elizabeth present at the manger? These B-players emerge as extras in God's story, but could it be they have significantly more to teach us about the intersection of God's story with ours? I wonder if perhaps we might find ourselves in these characters exactly because they are not so picture-perfect. They seem more accessible, more real, and grittier than the Holy Family.

Real life! Real life is what I am after in this Advent journey. I want to plumb the depths of these other characters to understand their experience and how it might relate to ours. Even with centuries separating us, could these Advent sidekicks teach us about hope, love, joy, and peace? I believe they can. Today we start this journey with dreams.

God-Sized Dreams

God puts dreams in all of us. It's just that sometimes we find ourselves wavering, and we doubt the legitimacy of our dreams. You have a dream, a vision, a goal for your life, and in the waiting, you begin to wonder, is this even possible? Could this actually happen? Do I have what it takes?

Perhaps over the last few years you have forgotten *how* to dream. There have been plenty of pandemic problems, distance delays, and a grab bag of straight-up cancellations. And it is no wonder with so much loss of potential, profit, and people we love, dreaming again seems, well, like an exercise in disappointment. I am an optimist by nature. I have spent most of my life deciding against the odds to take the risk and dream forward. Even in the middle of the pandemic, I was dreaming about my future. I was ready for a change—at least a change in scenery. That's when I started talking with my mom about my plans for the future.

I asked my mom if she would consider taking a trip with me. It was January 2021, and I was dreaming of a place and space with a bit more sunshine, maybe a beach, or at least a beautiful body of water. January in Ohio is nearly always a shade of gray and I needed sunshine! And truth be told, I wanted to get away and escape pandemic life. My mom quickly said she was not interested in any of that, dashing my dreams for fun in the sun. She piped up and said, "Rachel, I am determined to go to the Holy Land before I die. It's at the top of my bucket list."

"The Holy Land?" I questioned.

"Yes, the Holy Land," she said with dogged determination. "I'm not interested in going anywhere else!" Okay, Mom, tell me what you really think!

"Who knows, Mom?" I piped back, "those kinds of opportunities come up from time to time for pastor types. Maybe we could go sooner than later."

"You know, Rachel," my mom said wistfully. "I've always wanted to be a missionary, but I guess it was not in the cards."

"Yes, Mom, I know," I answered.

Now, somehow this trip of a lifetime to the Holy Land would be tied to my mother's calling as a Christian who traveled throughout the globe on behalf of God. For my mom, being a missionary had seemed like a dream beyond her reach. As a teenager who gave her life to Jesus, she had aspirations of serving God throughout the globe. But those dreams just seemed impossible.

For starters my mom had not flown on a plane since the summer of 1972 when she visited my dad while he was at Lackland Air Force base in San Antonio, Texas. My dad served in the United States Air Force, and they were soon to be engaged.

It was young love, and Linda Lou overcame her fear of flying just to see my father. It was the one time in her life that she boarded a plane. My mom is not exactly the traveling type. She has not spent a lot of time beyond the boundaries of Hocking County, Ohio.

Do not misunderstand what I am saying about my momma. She has the desire! These God dreams are in her heart. It is just that sometimes life happens, plans change, and those dreams—well, they are all but dashed. And sometimes people feel like they must give up on their dreams. My mom could not conceive of the combination of raising a family and working for God.

Giving Up on Your Dreams

Perhaps you have a dream that has lived rent-free in your head and heart for a long time. You dreamed of a career practicing international law. Maybe you believed you would live in a space and place more luxurious, or at least warmer. You had plans for relationships, for marriage, for children, but it just did not seem like it was in the stars. You had a vision for yourself, your family, your community, or even the world, and well, it just didn't take shape.

> Waiting is active waiting with minds, ears, and hearts leaning in, tilted toward a hope-filled future.

Advent is a season of waiting, but do not for a second think that this kind of waiting is a passive activity. Waiting is anything but passive. Even for you worrying types. Waiting is active waiting with minds, ears, and hearts leaning in, tilted toward a hope-filled future. We actively wait, placing our trust and lives in God's hands. And in this season of waiting, actively waiting for the coming Christ, we are a people of audacious hope.

In Advent we expect the unexpected. The atmosphere is ripe for dreaming! And yet for many of us it is difficult to get ourselves through the pessimism of past problems, political pressures, family frustrations, and dreams deferred in order to hope for the future.

And we are not alone. There are people in the Advent story who found themselves in a similar situation. Giving up on their dreams, they became steeped in a world of reality. What is actually possible in our ordinary lives? This was Zechariah and Elizabeth's story. They had hopes and dreams for their future. Family seemed to be part of the formula, but the Bible tell us that they just never had children of their own.

The Gospel of Luke tells the story of Zechariah and Elizabeth. They are not mentioned in Matthew, Mark, or John. Luke's telling of the Advent story is just a shade different than that of Matthew. For starters, Luke wanted the reader to know who was in charge, who was seemingly in power. It was Herod the Great and a variety of others in the political atmosphere. Certainly, Luke himself seemed heavily influenced by the Roman way of life, until he wrote of his encounters with this Jew named Jesus that set the whole world on fire with the presence of God:

> In the time of Herod king of Judea there was a priest named Zechariah, who belonged to the priestly division of Abijah; his wife Elizabeth was also a descendant of Aaron. Both of them were righteous in the sight of God, observing all the Lord's commands and decrees blamelessly. But they were childless

because Elizabeth was not able to conceive, and they were both very old. Once when Zechariah's division was on duty and he was serving as priest before God, he was chosen by lot, according to the custom of the priesthood, to go into the temple of the Lord and burn incense. And when the time for the burning of incense came, all the assembled worshipers were praying outside.

Luke 1:5-10

I imagine many of us have felt like Zechariah and Elizabeth. You had a vision and dream for your life and for whatever reason it just did not turn out the way you'd hoped. I imagine that through the decades this faith-filled couple was wondering, *What if we missed it?* They might have wondered if they missed their chance at having a family. Perhaps you have asked yourself a question. What if I missed my shot? What if I missed my opportunity of a good life? What if I missed out on a decent career? What if I missed a solid relationship? What if I missed it?

The past has a funny way of playing tricks on our future. Too often we romanticize the past and ignore the possibilities of the present. Anytime my husband, Jon, begins to talk about his high school or college football days, I tease him by calling out "glory days." He seems to fawn over the excitement of the past. But the truth is I too have fond memories of high school teammates and college races.

In the summer of 2022, I found myself sorting through boxes of trophies and banners from high school and college. It had been eight years since I had placed those boxes in an upstairs attic, and I had all but forgotten they were there. Eight years spent at Ginghamsburg Church felt like a crucible of leadership. We navigated through beautifully horrific leadership transitions, devastating storms, a mass shooting in Dayton, Ohio, and the crushing pressures of COVID-19. And near the tail end of that journey, we came to the other side to a diagnosis for our youngest child, the single most precious addition to our family in those eight years.

Sarah was diagnosed with Marfan syndrome, a rare genetic disorder that affects all the connective tissue in her body. Marfan syndrome had somehow randomly invaded her DNA. My husband took her to see a pediatric ophthalmologist. Her regular eye doctor was concerned about the cloudiness in our then five-year-old's eyes. "She may have cataracts," the doctor remarked.

"Cataracts?" I questioned.

It seemed impossible for a tiny child to have cataracts. She reassured my husband and me that it was possible. It was spring break, and my teacher husband took her to the appointment. They waited for what seemed like forever to see the doctor. So, when my husband texted, "doc believes Sarah has Marfan syndrome." I was relieved. We have a possible answer!

"Rachel, did you Google that?" Jon texted back.

No, I had not Googled it. But when I did, I was a puddle on the ground. Not only could the disease affect her eyesight, but also every single piece of connective tissue in her body, including her heart.

While it was not the exact reason for my packing my belongings and family and moving halfway across the state of Ohio, her diagnosis was the tipping point. All the future dreams I had for Ginghamsburg Church and my family were deferred. Sarah would not be deterred. That bundle of joy, all five years of her, was eager to step into Momma's past and sort through my attic boxes.

For Sarah, this seemed like a treasure chest of discovery, a version of her mother she did not quite understand and a version of myself I had nearly forgotten. There were running plaques and medals, an assortment of slides for my art portfolio as I had contemplated colleges of design. There were seven academic achievement awards I had zero recollection of receiving. No wonder I had so much trouble attempting to figure out what I was supposed to do with my life! Those were the glory days: high school academic achievements, medals won, and pictures drawn.

"Mommy, I didn't know you were an artist!" Sarah declared.

"I was," I remarked as she sorted through the paintings in my high school portfolio. These were and are my dreams deferred. Some days I still dream of being an artist, and yet it just does not seem to be in the cards. We totally can honor the past and celebrate our achievements. But when the past becomes the pinnacle of the present, we find ourselves paralyzed, staring into a future without possibilities. Moving is not easy, because it means change. And change is challenging.

One Sunday afternoon, I was listening to National Public Radio where a neuroscientist was talking about our resistance to change. Even though our brains are constantly changing as we grow and develop, we human types tend to resist changing our minds. Our brains develop these neural pathways and they become content with what they know. It's like the well-worn path in the woods or ruts that have been created driving the tractor between farm fields and buildings. The ruts get deep and it's difficult to walk any other way. Like the ruts, these neural pathways get static. It's hard for our brains to want to change. Hard, but not impossible!

Sometimes we want to hold on to stories or narratives that make sense of our lives: the good, the bad, and the in-between. They are comfortable. These stories that we tell ourselves are what we know. And our brains sort of hold on to them. We resist changing our minds. Our stories shape our identities. But when our stories distort our reality, they can keep us from moving forward. Friend, does it have to be that way? What happens when our life narrative becomes a barrier to our future? What happens if we refuse to change? We get stuck! And often fear is fueling that paralysis.

> Sometimes we want to hold on to stories or narratives that make sense of our lives: the good, the bad, and the in-between. They are comfortable. These stories that we tell ourselves are what we know.

Zechariah was stuck as well. And it took God showing up in Zechariah's life to get him unstuck. Zechariah was one of a number of priests who served in Jerusalem at the Temple. The Temple took center stage in the lives of God's people in Jerusalem. Each priest served one week in the Temple twice a year. Zechariah was performing his priestly duties when it happened that he was chosen by lot to burn incense in the Holy of Holies. This meant a once-in-a-lifetime trip into this sacred space. Not every priest was afforded the opportunity for this special service, and a priest could only be selected once in his entire life. Zechariah was not going to miss that shot.

The process for burning incense was not complicated. Sure, there were very specific instructions: prayers to pray, incense to light, and a benediction to give the listeners in the Temple that day.

11

The benediction was the sign that the ceremony was complete. It was an honor, and yet the ritual was simple and quick. Zechariah should have been in and out. But it was not simple and quick, not this time. Luke wrote that while Zechariah was performing the priestly rituals an angel of the Lord stood at the right side of the altar of incense. Can you imagine? A divine being just shows up unannounced in the middle of your unlikely story? Now I know we have these cute pictures of chubby cherubs in our mind, particularly when thinking of a story as sacred as the Christmas story. But angels seem to be anything but cute. Nearly every time a messenger of the Lord shows up unannounced people are afraid. Luke tells us:

> *When Zechariah saw him, he was startled and was gripped with fear. But the angel said to him: "Do not be afraid, Zechariah; your prayer has been heard. Your wife Elizabeth will bear you a son, and you are to call him John. He will be a joy and delight to you, and many will rejoice because of his birth, for he will be great in the sight of the Lord. He is never to take wine or other fermented drink, and he will be filled with the Holy Spirit even before he is born. He will bring back many of the people of Israel to the Lord their God. And he will go on before the Lord, in the spirit and power of Elijah, to turn the hearts of the parents to their children and the disobedient to the wisdom of the righteous—to make ready a people prepared for the Lord."*
>
> *Luke 1:12-17*

Certainly, that was not the announcement that Zechariah expected to receive that day in the Temple. He was gripped with fear. Whatever he witnessed terrified him to his core! I imagine many of us do not expect the God of the universe to show up at our workplace, and if God did, we too would be paralyzed with fear. Zechariah questioned, How can I be sure of this? He did the math. He was old and his wife more seasoned as well (notice in the Scripture Zechariah did not claim that Elizabeth was old. Good man, Zechariah! Good man! Choose your words carefully!). Zechariah was overwhelmed, unsure, really skeptical about what the angel of the Lord was telling him. How was this even possible?

Scared Speechless

The moment that God's messenger appears to Zechariah, Zechariah was scared out of his mind. Perhaps he never expected God to show up, not in that way. I mean, Zechariah was in the most religious spot on the face of the planet, the Holy of Holies. But even religious types do not necessarily expect God to show up so profoundly and so personally.

Let's be honest, sometimes we too get so caught up in the religious routine that we forget to expect the unexpected. While we are worshipping week after week, we can become numb to certain God possibilities. Of course, we believe with God all things are possible. It is just that sometimes we do not imagine those possibilities are for us, our community, our church, our families, and ourselves. God shows up for other people all the time, but for us we are not so sure. We cling to the reality that is consistent, if not comforting. We begin to buy into the lie that we are the makers of our own destiny and that if God's power and presence are part of the equation, it's only demonstrated through our own constant faithfulness. We have to be faithful for God to show up.

Zechariah and Elizabeth were certainly faithful. They followed the law and held on to a faith that kept them bound beautifully to community. Consistency is rarely a bad way to live. And yet something in the narrative, something in the regular routine blinded Zechariah to a future that could be different from his comforting norm. And fear has a funny way of squelching expectations. Fear has a way of paralyzing our present.

What was Zechariah scared speechless about? Suddenly he couldn't talk at all. Even though he was disciplined, and by all accounts he and his wife lived by the spirit of love, could it be that Zechariah did not see beyond what was right in front of him. He and his wife were childless, but this was about more than his immediate family. Zechariah's people, his tribe, the community that held his identity was occupied and oppressed by the likes of the Roman Empire. They were living into the reality that occupation was right out their front door.

Perhaps his fear was masking the hopelessness he felt. Hopeless because there was not a clear path forward for himself or God's people. Maybe lament was the only vocabulary that seemed reasonable as Zechariah stepped into the Holy of Holies that day. I encounter people all the time who believe in God, but sometimes they do not believe in themselves. At the very least they are not expecting God to show up in their ordinary lives anytime soon. They have experienced too much pain to believe that God is present in their lives.

> Sometimes when hope is unclear, God illumines a path, a dream forward.

And in that moment of Zechariah's life, it seemed that too much time had passed between prophetic messages and the present. God's revelation seemed like a spiritual currency that had all but dried up. And the best work that Zechariah could muster was to show up. Zechariah kept praying, continued to believe, and moved forward even when the future seemed a bit too hard, too limited to expect the unexpected. Perhaps the fear was the result of a dream dimmed by this suffering. How could he even begin to dream forward? Perhaps if he had just remembered God's movement in the past—the way that God moved through God's people. Sometimes when hope is unclear, God illumines a path, a dream forward.

Cracks Are Where the Light Floods In

It is our human tendency to want to smooth over the rough edges of our story. Let us just eliminate all the confusions and pain. But what if the pain and confusion are only new ways we can see the beauty and experience the good? What if we understood that good wins when the light breaks through the cracks of our human experience? When we scroll through our news feeds it is difficult to reconcile the day-to-day struggles of life and a hopeful future. We need a bigger picture, a broader plan to make sense of our human experience.

This is why we are united by a single human family. Our story begins in the Book of Genesis. In fact, that is what the word *genesis* means, the beginning. Zechariah was a priest, and it is presumable to believe that he knew God's bigger story. This was the story of God of the universe choosing a single family to draw back to God. Three major religions, Judaism, Christianity, and Islam, point to this family as their origin story. This promise of a new way to be family, a new way to be human, and a new way to move forward gave Zechariah and Elizabeth the hope that their dreams were possible!

So, God chose a couple, first known as Abram and Sarai and later renamed Abraham and Sarah to birth his people. This couple had traveled from the land that they knew, Ur, to a foreign land called Canaan. When Abraham and Sarah stepped into the dream, God was determined to make their family and their descendants what is described in Genesis 12:2: "I will make you into a great nation, and I will bless you; I will make your name great, and you will be a blessing."

There was just one small problem: Abraham and Sarah had zero children at the time. Does that sound familiar? Abraham and Sarah have parallel lives and stories to that of Zechariah and Elizabeth. And it had been twenty-five years since Abraham and Sarah made that move from Ur to Canaan. You can imagine that they are deeply sad, skeptical, and frustrated. Abraham and Sarah may even feel a bit forgotten. If you had traveled to a place you had never been, without family or community, perhaps you too would have wondered, *Where are you God?* I imagine many of you, particularly those in ministry, have made a similar move. I know I have had moments when I thought to myself, *Are you sure, God? I am not sure I signed up for this!* When life becomes overwhelming it can be difficult not to question the decisions we have made.

Abraham and Sarah did what most human beings attempt to do when future dreams and plans are not going our way. We attempt to make life happen ourselves. Sometimes in our grief, we aggressively try to take control. Abraham and Sarah rush the promise, and in the process they abused a slave girl, Hagar. Hagar birthed a potential heir. Sarah perceived Hagar and her precious baby, Ishmael, as a threat. It is the kind of Bible story that fills your heart and head with sorrow, wondering, *why would Abraham and Sarah do such a thing?*

It is in this season of pain and disappointment that we find God paying Abraham and Sarah a visit. Three messengers of God appear to Abraham and Sarah near the great trees of Mamre. Abraham was minding his own business in the middle of the day when suddenly three figures appeared.

Abraham hurried to offer the three messengers hospitality.

> *"If I have found favor in your eyes, my lord, do not pass your servant by. Let a little water be brought, and then you may all wash your feet and rest under this tree. Let me get you something to eat, so you can be refreshed and then go on your way—now that you have come to your servant." "Very well,"* *they answered, "do as you say."*
>
> Genesis 18:3-5

It's the cracks in your life that allow the light to shine in. Abraham and Sarah have some major work to do in their relationship, in reconciliation, and in justice. And yet in the middle of their mess, three messengers come to visit. It was interesting that right off the bat, Abraham calls these visitors "my lord." It was unclear as to whether the visitors are angels or human manifestations of God, but these three strangers have a holy mission, and somehow Abraham saw their potentially divine destiny. God has gathered at Abraham's table.

Let us be clear, hospitality is a big deal among the Hebrew people. It is not a bonus. Hospitality is not nice exchange between friends or even charging a fee for a stranger. Hospitality was understood as a way of life for God's people. As we read through the Old Testament, we experience God's presence through bread, sacrifice, meals, community, and family. There was always room around the table for family, but also for the stranger, the orphan, the immigrant, and the widow. The Old Testament language is strong concerning hospitality to those on the margins: "Cursed is anyone who withholds justice from the foreigner, the fatherless or the widow" (Deuteronomy 27:19).

And even in the New Testament there is this pull to welcoming in the stranger. Jesus himself said, "I was a stranger and you invited me in" (Matthew 25:35b). And in Hebrews 13 the writer declares, "Do not forget to show hospitality to strangers, for by so doing some people have shown hospitality to angels without knowing it" (Hebrews 13:2). God has a habit of making room even for the messiest of human beings. But this is no mere dinner party. It's a party with a purpose.

Abraham asked his wife Sarah to help him with these preparations. Abraham was ready to roll out the red carpet for these messengers. He gave very specific instructions to knead and bake bread and to select the finest calf for butcher and preparation. And oh, do not forget the milk and curds! These strangers were going to have to wait a minute for the meal to be ready for their consumption. But the waiting gave Abraham the opportunity to be in conversation with these divine visitors. "'Where is your wife Sarah?' they asked him. 'There, in the tent,' he said. Then one of them said, 'I will surely return to you about this time next year, and Sarah your wife will have a son'" (Genesis 18:9-10).

This is no simple DoorDash! Abraham was pulling out all the stops for these strangers and they have a clear message for him. Do you remember the promise? The one that inspired you to leave everything you have ever known and travel to a foreign country to become God's people? Abraham, do you remember that promise?

I know it has been a long time coming. I know you have wondered if God had forgotten you. But God has not forgotten you.

Can you imagine how Abraham and Sarah must have been treated? Of course, they have doubt! Couple those doubts with gossip as the neighbors started to question why they moved so far in the first place. These neighbors are dream crushers: Why would these strangers inhabit our land? Is their so-called god going to help them now? Abraham and Sarah have boasted that they are going to be the mother and father of nations, and so far, they have zero children. They are either simply foolish or downright mad.

Perhaps you have been there. You have believed that the move in location, career, in relationship was good, and maybe you thought you heard God. But time passed with no clear confirmation and the silence has you questioning, *Was that you, God, or something strange that I ate? What do I do with this dream now?*

> Perhaps your story is not an exact match with their story, but certainly themes of our human condition begin to emerge. Themes of hope, dreams deferred, trust, abandonment, and dependence. We are only human after all.

Abraham and Sarah are hanging on by their fingernails to a promise they barely remember receiving. Do you hear why this story is so important? Are you beginning to hear your own unlikely story in the story of Abraham and Sarah? Are you seeing yourselves in Zechariah and Elizabeth? Perhaps your story is not an exact match with their story, but certainly themes of our human condition begin to emerge. Themes of hope, dreams deferred, trust, abandonment, and dependence. We are only human after all.

But God's story does not stop there and neither does the story of Abraham and Sarah. Sarah seems to be listening from the tent the entire time. She was curious about these visitors. And she recognized the limitations of her age and Abraham's as well. So she laughed at the thought of her giving birth to a child at her age.

> *"After I am worn out and my lord is old, will I now have this pleasure?" Then the LORD said to Abraham, "Why did Sarah laugh and say, 'Will I really have a child, now that I am old?' Is anything too hard for the LORD? I will return to you at the appointed time next year, and Sarah will have a son." Sarah was afraid, so she lied and said, "I did not laugh." But he said, "Yes, you did laugh."*
>
> Genesis 18:12b-15

I can so relate to this. Why is it that when we get caught doing something we should not have done our first response is usually to hide? We come by that honestly, don't we? When Adam and Eve did the very thing that God told them not to do, they hid from God. And in their hiding, shame reared its ugly head. They were naked and afraid. They did not want to face God.

> *But the LORD God called to the man, "Where are you?" He answered, "I heard you in the garden, and I was afraid because I was naked; so I hid." And he said, "Who told you that you were naked? Have you eaten from the tree that I commanded you not to eat from?"*
>
> Genesis 3:9-11

When humans feel shame, we tend to hide and deny. Now I am not convinced that the angel was chastising Sarah for laughing. I believe this messenger just wanted to be clear, "You laughed Sarah, but the promise is still valid. Your laughing is not going to deter God from doing what God has already promised. God's dream for you is still alive!" And before we blame Sarah too much for her laughter, remember that Abraham also laughed (Genesis 17:17).

And who can blame them? Their dream was given almost twenty-five years prior, and they were old when they received the promise. The fear, the pain, the longing, the hopelessness, is all a part of their story. I love this story because it is Abraham and Sarah's story, it is Zechariah and Elizabeth's story, it is God's story, and it is also our story.

Could it be that connecting the dots between the dreams of Abraham and Sarah, and Zechariah and Elizabeth, reminds us of the arc of history and God's amazing hopeful trajectory? Our story, our very messy and misunderstood human story, collides with our experience of the divine. You might be saying, *well, that is great for Abraham and Sarah, and Zechariah and Elizabeth. But that is not great news for me. I am struggling to dream forward.*

I imagine you too are doing your best to put one foot in front of the other. Perhaps you too have experienced a moment where fear has rendered you speechless. Maybe it was taking the certification exam and failing it for the third time. Or it was being overlooked for the job promotion when the bills were piling up. Maybe it was after you had taken too many pregnancy tests to count. During all of these times and more we have all but lost our ability to lean in to hope. But God specializes in the realm of the unlikely.

Set Your Hopes High

The angel Gabriel knows full well the prayers of God's people and commanded Zechariah not to be afraid. Why? Because God is getting ready to birth a new promise in and through Elizabeth and him. And that new promise had a name and a destiny. Zechariah and Elizabeth's son John (aka John the Baptist) would prepare God's people for the coming of the Messiah.

John had a clear job description. He's going to be a big deal. But John's purpose required sacrifice: no alcohol. John would be so full of the Holy Spirit that God did not want anyone to confuse his spiritual fervor with being drunk. His work would bring the people of Israel back to God. John would prepare the way of Jesus! The promise brought Zechariah fear, but not Elizabeth.

Elizabeth set her hopes high. She does not seem to fear, but also has experienced the pain of disappointment. Then one day, when it seemed like all hope was lost, her husband has an encounter with a messenger of God. Zechariah was confused. The messenger's announcement was unbelievable. Zechariah seemed doubtful, perhaps even skeptical, but not Elizabeth. Elizabeth did not seem to question. She certainly did not laugh like Abraham or Sarah, but rather rejoiced and spent time in joyful reflection. "'The Lord has done this for me,' she said. 'In these days he has shown his favor and taken away my disgrace among the people'" (Luke 1:25).

God has taken away Elizabeth's disgrace. When Elizabeth was about to give birth to her son, the community gathered. I imagine many people in the community milling around in anticipation of what will transpire. Who will this child be? How will Zechariah respond? Elizabeth gives birth to the child that she names John,

Hebrew for "God is gracious." Her disgrace was removed with God's grace. And yet the community that surrounded Elizabeth in her birthing experience seemed to disapprove. John was not a family name. Those surrounding Elizabeth asked Zechariah to weigh in. Zechariah was still unable to speak when the child was born. And yet when asked for the child's name, Zechariah wrote out the name John. And instantly, Zechariah was able to speak again!

Names are powerful. In this Advent season as you gather around tables, some with friends and others with family, will you set your hopes high or will you live into old names? Family sometimes asks us to carry names or labels that limit or even harm us. What name do you carry to the table? Perhaps you have picked up a name for yourself. Or maybe you have had a friend label you, or even the community you find yourself in. I hate to put it in writing, but even church folk are known to give people less than helpful names.

> So, let us set our hopes high. Living into Advent means living into the hope that good news is coming.

But let me remind you, you are not a disgrace, you are not the black sheep, you are not the loser, and you are not the deadbeat. Friend, you are clothed in grace. You are a beloved child of the living God. God still plants dreams in our heads and hearts. God invites us to move forward toward a hopeful future. God gives new names. So, let us set our hopes high. Living into Advent means living into the hope that good news is coming.

I cannot guarantee that you will have the opportunity to live out every dream you have ever had for your future. I certainly cannot predict whether every goal you have had for your life will be accomplished. But I can say this with conviction: living with a heavy dose of negativity is a crummy way to live. It is nearly a guarantee that fear will hold you hostage.

We have a choice to make: cling to the negativity that sometimes is pervasive in our lives or set our hopes high. Could we be disappointed? Absolutely! But people who live with a relentless, faith-filled optimism pave their own way into an unlikely story and offer others that same hope in the process. They inspire us to believe and live differently.

Dream Forward

We are able to dream forward! Throughout these pandemic years, I have encountered numerous people who have shifted jobs, changed careers, and questioned their entire vocations. They have been searching, longing for a bit of vocational guidance and hope. People are consulting everyone from spiritual directors to life coaches, counselors to even mystics to somehow figure out how to dream forward. I have a leadership coach, a message coach, and a therapist, because I want to be the healthiest version of myself. And I need help to dream forward.

I need other voices in my life calling out the dreams of the past and helping me paint a picture of a new future. You have dreams living inside of you. Some of those dreams are seemingly broken dreams from your past. Human beings can hold on to those past dreams with dogged determination. But could it be that there's life in the cracks of those broken dreams. Those broken bits when examined and rearranged are reformed to make something new. It reminds me of the Japanese art *kintsugi* where broken pottery is remade by binding the shattered pieces together with precious metals like gold. You can take those broken bits and, with help, dream again into the future.

Could it be that we've either held on so tightly to the broken bits of our dreams or even ignored them completely that we can't see new art emerging from the rubble?

At the core of who people are is not a desire for more power, but rather a deep need for more meaning. I wonder, are we church leaders teaching our people how to dream? Are we giving people the tools to dabble in a world of God possibilities? Do our people have permission to dream forward? For example, art does not have to be something that I leave on the shelf of my past dreams. What if I take my passion for art and apply it to the opportunities that God has already given me? Honestly I have this deep desire to begin sketching again, especially when I find myself hiking in the woods. I want to capture the beauty of God's good creation and replicate the experience on paper.

> But dreaming is not a season. People of all ages and stages are designed to dream forward.

Am I scared? Of course. My perfectionism sometimes chokes out my ability to dream forward because I am afraid I will not be good enough. Maybe that's your story. So many people are wondering if they are enough. They believe they are too old, too young, too tired, that life has passed them by, and they should step out of the dreaming season of their life. You can hear Zechariah's voice protesting that he is not enough as he questions the angel of the Lord. I am too old for this, God. But dreaming is not a season. People of all ages and stages are designed to dream forward.

We have our own version of life coaching in the church. We call it discipleship. This looks like Jesus followers helping other Jesus followers paint a God-centered picture for their future. We need one another to call out the dreams we see in each other. We need a messenger to say, Do not be afraid, God is with you. You can do this. You can dream forward, we can dream into the future together.

Could it be that we struggle to help people dream forward because we too have lost hope. Church as we knew it has changed: online, in-person, and hybrid experiences challenged our pictures of the church. There is a seeming acceleration of the loss of people and influence in the communities we find ourselves in. Even if your local expression of church is growing, what "worked" before has lost its effectiveness. Each of these challenges is a barrier to dreaming into the future.

The church of the future is going to be different. What great news! Different can be oh-so-good. I want to be a leader who gives people permission to dream. When we give people permission to dream, we experience church as a world of possibilities. It's like a sandbox. When you are making a castle in a sandbox, you know it's not going to last forever, but you give yourself permission to play, create, and dream of new worlds of possibility. Could we become spaces and places where people are given permission to play? Could churches gift our people with permission to try and fail and try and fail? Could we be dream builders rather than dream crushers? Do not cling to what was but rather let us dream forward together.

Contagious Hope

Dreaming forward requires contagious hope. When my mom and I rescheduled our trip to the Holy Land for late summer 2022, I was less than optimistic. Our trip had been canceled four times. In fact, I said to myself, until we land in Tel Aviv, I'm not going to believe we are actually going to the Holy Land. But in August, Mom and I packed our bags and headed for the airport. Our hope was reignited! We made our way from Dallas to Frankfurt and finally landed in Israel. A baggage delay gave my mom and me plenty of time to regroup and hang with our tour guide. Ordinary delays and disappointments are fertile ground for God to do an unlikely work.

Sitting in the lobby with a lox sandwich and Turkish coffee in hand, I felt like a kid in a candy store. Who receives hours of one-on-one attention from your guide before the trip even truly begins? At first we made small talk, but then I decided to interview our guide. We went deep quickly. We talked at length about the Palestinian-Israeli conflict. David was a Palestinian Christian, a brother in Christ. I had questions about American exceptionalism, that is, the belief that the United States is particular and special in the world, and how many people who travel to the Holy Land come with a false sense of a grandiose self. I also asked him about his life, faith, and his perceptions of Christianity particularly in the United States.

David talked about a lack of humility. That some American Christians have gone as far as to decide who is in and who is out because we have made ourselves out to be God. That stung a little. I was curious and so I asked, "David, what frustrates you the most about Christians in the United States?"

27

"Blind faith," he responded. "Hatred is fueled by blind faith."

Certainly, there are a host of opinions and political conversations swirling around the Middle East conflict. So, when I asked David if he was afraid of living in Israel, he said no. He was not afraid. Sure, David had family hurt and even killed in the conflict, yet he was not afraid.

His response surprised me. If I lived in this kind of daily tension, I would live in fear. His determination was inspiring. His disposition was so hopeful. I asked, "So then, David, what gives you such hope?"

"I find hope in change," he said. "When people come and experience this land for what it is, the people for who they are, when others come and see our land with their own eyes and their minds are changed. It gives me hope! Change gives me hope."

We are going to have to work to change our minds. Change is challenging. And yet followers of Jesus are going to have to change to give people hope!

> In order to help one another dream forward, to dream new God possibilities, hope is the first step.

Hope is contagious. The angel infused Zechariah and Elizabeth, and by extension God's people, with hope. We need hope. In order to help one another dream forward, to dream new God possibilities, hope is the first step. When we listen to one another's stories, when we feel each other's suffering, we see a new generation of Jesus followers weed through all the political jargon and have the courage to see people as people. It gifts us hope and, in the process, we are changed. We begin to believe that if

God can rewrite the stories of other people, God can rewrite our unlikely stories as well. We become a birthplace of hope. Hope is what we all long for. Hope that dreaming again is possible. Hope that the future can and will look different. Hope that we can learn to trust again. Hope for a new story. Trust that God can rewrite our unlikely stories.

Your Unlikely Story

God specializes in unlikely stories. God met an old man in the middle of a sacred space to open his heart and his eyes to new dreams for him, Elizabeth, and God's people. God gave Zechariah the entire time of Elizabeth's pregnancy to remember God's promises for the future, to reclaim broken dreams, and to be ready to dream forward. If God can rewrite their unlikely story, God can rewrite ours as well. But if we are not careful, we can miss it.

We miss future dreams by holding on to the broken bits, by losing our imaginations, and by refusing to have our minds changed. It's scary to dream forward like Zechariah and Elizabeth. What if something bad happens? What if life doesn't work out? Fear paralyzes us, robbing us of our potential, destroying new possibilities, and leaving us with old anxieties. But God has not given us a spirit of fear, but a spirit of power, love, and self-discipline. We have not missed it! God is still at work, writing an unlikely story in you.

Ageism is real, but God's plan has no end date. Infertility is a dream crusher, but God weaves new and creative possibilities. Perhaps you are a person whose finances seem futile, but God can make a way where there seems to be no way. You put a name on

29

yourself, "I am not enough," but the God of all wisdom is your salvation. Your dreams may feel unimportant, but God's path moves way beyond what you can hope or imagine. Dreaming forward feels too risky, but Jesus says, "It is I; don't be afraid" (John 6:20). You are afraid that you messed everything up, but the people walking in darkness have seen a great light. You do not know where to start, and yet Jesus invites all who are weary and weighed down to simply come to him. Let God rewrite your unlikely story. Dream again!

God is no cosmic Santa Claus. Humans do not receive everything we have ever wanted, yet there are dreams in our head and in our hearts that God wants to creatively partner with us to make happen. What are you dreaming about these days? What could happen with an innovative partnership? What dreams could come to fruition? Could you become a person of possibility? Could your church and its leadership give people permission to play? Whether you are twelve, twenty-two, or the age of Zechariah and Elizabeth, there is a God possibility in each one of us. It is time for us in this Advent season to let God rewrite our unlikely stories.

2

Playing
the Villain

Chapter 2

PLAYING THE VILLAIN

Ever get skeptical about real life relationships? Friendships sometimes seem difficult, particularly in adulthood. The older we get, the more difficult it is to have deep, meaningful friendships. Perhaps it is because we are exposed to fewer new people, or maybe we are limited by our own personality types. For whatever reason, we adult types regularly struggle with healthy friendships.

And yet through the pages of Scripture we read about a God who made us for relationship with God and one another. We need people. This is why I have grown to greatly appreciate the connection with my covenant group. Our covenant group is a small group of clergywomen who meet every other week for encouragement and accountability. We have been gathering for over a decade. These women are my lifeline.

Last November we were discussing Advent as preacher types tend to do, and I could not help myself. I had to share this idea of an unlikely Advent and the characters in the Advent narrative that do not take center stage. Of course, the Nativity points to stories of Mary, Joseph, and the baby Jesus, but what about Zechariah and Elizabeth? And no one includes Herod.

> ## You and I realize there is a reason King Herod is not included in our standard Nativity sets.

That's when one of my pastor friends piped up and said that a young boy in her congregation felt the same way. He decided to give her a Herod figurine to add to her Nativity collection that year. When she texted us the picture, I thought the Herod figurine had a strange resemblance to the "The Burger King." I laughed out loud, but it was the thought that counts. The little guy was asking the same question that I am asking, "Why doesn't anyone include Herod in the Nativity scene?" The kid is right! We should get ourselves a Herod. But you and I realize there is a reason King Herod is not included in our standard Nativity sets.

Nobody Loves a Villain

We've got the likes of the Marvel Universe and DC comics to thank for our indoctrination in all things villainous. Thanos, Loki, Ultron, The Joker, Lex Luthor, and Bane are a few of the bad guys. And it's not merely comic book series; nearly every Disney princess movie provides a generation with a villain to despise. I know it takes a solid antagonist to craft a good story, but when we shade every character into bad and good categories it robs us and new generations of the nuances of the human condition. What do I mean?

When traveling in the Holy Land with my mom, we found ourselves perched on top of Masada, Herod the Great's desert fortress. The landscape is grandiose. The 1,300-foot climb to the top of the plateau is not exactly a walk in the park. But I love a good challenge, and I wanted to get my steps in for the day. The challenge was calling my name. But although I wanted to climb the stairs to make it to the top, our guide David insisted that the 100-degree temperatures would be deterrent enough to keep us from that kind of rigorous exercise. Besides, David said, "You want to see what's up there, don't you? Rachel, you don't have time for both the climb and the viewing!"

I was disappointed, but I knew he was right. And I did want to see what was on the top of that plateau that spanned nearly thirty acres. We patiently waited our turn to ride the gondola to the top. We were making small talk until we began the ascent. I was glued to the glass doors as we rose. The higher we climbed, so did my heart rate, and the less disappointed I became. It was high, really high! I realized, maybe, just maybe I would not have made it to the top after all. Once the gondola was in its resting position, I was quick to exit and place my feet firmly on the ground. "Welcome to Masada," David said with a wide smile.

Perhaps by unpacking the history of this place we could better understand our villain. There is quite a bit of controversy surrounding Masada, from being the last stronghold of the Jewish rebellion against the Roman Empire to the oppression baked into its construction. There is an eeriness to the land. That eeriness raises the question, What actually happened here?

Flavius Josephus, the first-century Jewish historian, attributed the grandiose palaces and their construction to Herod the Great. And the archeological elevations of Yigael Yadin confirm his claim.[1] Remnants of colorful mosaics and stucco-walls reveal glimpses of a glorious past. More impressive than the palaces, porches, food storage, and bathhouses are the water cisterns. Water from the mountains made its way through simple and yet profound irrigation designs into these cisterns. However, it's unclear as to whether Herod and his family ever actually lived at Masada.

It was not until years later that Jewish rebels, known as the Sicarii, "dagger-men," laid claim to the fortress. Masada became the last foothold of the First Jewish Revolt against the Romans. Josephus recorded that nearly a thousand men, women, and children occupied Masada after the destruction of Jerusalem in 70 CE. And the Tenth Roman legion arrived at the foot of the fortress in 73 or 74 CE. Although well supplied, the Roman legion was determined to attack the mountain.

Here is where the tale takes an interesting turn. Josephus recorded that the Roman army built a ramp up the western slope of the plateau. When breaching of the fortress seemed inevitable, Jewish leader Eleazar ben Ya'ir led his men and their families in a massive suicide pact: each man was to kill his own family, and then ten men chosen by lot to kill the others, until one lone survivor would kill himself.[2] Did this happen? Or was this some kind of fairy tale conscripted by Josephus himself with pressure from Rome? It is a bit mysterious. What is clear is that people died, leaving a mark in Jewish and Roman history. That level of violence leaves a mark on a place. Masada was and is the kind of place where death seemed to seep into the rocky ground.

As our tour group made our way to the pinnacle of Herod's living quarters, we found ourselves overlooking the landscape from what would have been the veranda. The view was majestic. And the height had my stomach churning. Did I mention it was high? And then it hit me: Herod himself could have stood in the very place I was standing. In that moment there was this feeling of awe that came over me. Imagine being the king of Judea overlooking this valley with the power and privilege of Rome in your corner. And for a moment I realized the pull of power and the seduction of influence. Perched on top of Masada I realized there was a little Herod in me. There is a little Herod in all of us.

> **Perched on top of Masada I realized there was a little Herod in me. There is a little Herod in all of us.**

The author of the Gospel of Matthew had a point. He was attempting to help his hearers make a connection between the life, death, and resurrection of Jesus, and God's work throughout the Old Testament. Matthew placed Jesus in the long lineage of men and some women who had been "A" players in God's plan of salvation. Jesus is in the lineage of Father Abraham and Mother Sarah. Jesus was a new teacher like Moses; but more than his family tree and style of teaching, Jesus was *Immanuel:* God with us.

And how does God decide to, as the Gospel of John narrates it, "[become] flesh and blood and [move] into the neighborhood" (John 1:14, MSG)? It was surprising. Jesus was not born in a palace. His birth did not take place among the likes of Herod and his family. Nor did Jesus have the backing of the Roman Empire. Jesus could not lay claim to that power and privilege.

God came to us as a Jewish baby born into a family with limited material resources. His birth took place in a stable, possibly a cave-like structure. The birth of Jesus was relegated to a portion of a first-century home that housed animals and offered limited medical attention to the birthing mother. It was a challenging place to have a baby, let alone the Savior of the world.

Mary and Joseph seem vulnerable. They were not exactly a power couple by yesterday's or today's standards. And yet the God of the universe made strength available to all of us who lack power, privilege, and resources through the birth of this God child. Power as a helpless baby wrapped in a simple cloth, the opposite of me as I stood on a plateau at Masada. Jesus represented a new definition of power and influence.

And into this context, Matthew told the story of magi from the east coming to Jerusalem. These men were searching for something mysterious. They had been studying the sky, and by their calculations, a king was coming to the Jews. They were so determined, so sure of their astrological discernment that they came all the way to Judea to visit Herod the Great. It was a bold move, compelled by compassion and perhaps divine destiny.

They ask, "Where is the one who has been born king of the Jews?" These learned men are so bold as to say they have seen the star for themselves and are ready to worship this new king. Herod was shocked. He immediately gathered groups of his learned men to give him answers. He called together the chief priest and teachers of the law, questioning if this were possible. Could it be true? Where is the Messiah to be born?

Herod recognized the limitations of his power and privilege. He may be king, but Herod the Great was not a messiah. The chief priest and the teachers of the law knew the Scriptures and quickly replied, "In Bethlehem in Judea." In that moment, it seemed as though Herod had just discovered the exact coordinates of a threat, because he was quick to share the information with the magi. Skilled in making backroom deals and political alliances, Herod asked the magi to do him a solid. Please seek out the child and report your findings back to me, "so that I too may go and worship him" (Matthew 2:8).

Herod was disturbed and paranoid. Herod did what he does best, which was to start manipulating the situation. Herod perceived this so-called king of the Jews a threat to his power and privilege. And it's no wonder. History tells us that Herod the Great lived a contentious life. From the beginning of his political career, Herod was always fighting to retain his power and authority. Twice Jewish authorities from Jerusalem asked for his removal, but Hyrcanus II kept Herod and his brother Phasael in their positions.[3]

Herod was not exactly popular among the people. And yet the opposition to Herod's rule of Jewish territory was not limited to the people there. Many throughout the Roman Empire opposed Herod the Great. He stood trial on several occasions, and his own mother-in-law attempted to seize positions in Jerusalem. So, what did Herod do? He had all those who opposed him executed, including his own flesh and blood.

Cruel, paranoid, and seemingly senseless in his violence, Herod lived by the myth of redemptive violence and believed that the strongest arm ruled by divine destiny. His belief was that he could fight his way into being and doing right—the strongest arm not only rules but wins because the cosmos has determined it to be so. Herod's marriage to violence was a union forged in *Pax Romana*, Roman Peace.

Roman peace guaranteed stability for occupied nations, if and only if they played by the rules of the Roman Empire. There was a reason that Herod and all of Jerusalem were disturbed when the magi arrived. The arrival of foreign officials could not end well. There was not room in Herod's Judea for other powers, players, or opinions. Fear was the currency of the powerful, and it was invested in manipulating people. Herod determined manipulation of the magi was the best way to get them to do his bidding.

According to Matthew's Gospel, after Herod learned that the magi had rejected his request, he was angry. So angry that he was willing to kill every male child in Bethlehem under the age of two. Herod took a leap from homicide to genocide fueled by his clinging to political power.

> Then what was said through the prophet Jeremiah was fulfilled:
> "A voice is heard in Ramah, weeping and great mourning,
> Rachel weeping for her children and refusing to be comforted,
> because they are no more."
>
> Matthew 2:17-18

Did the genocide of a lot of innocent children happen? The historical evidence of such an act was unclear, but these actions certainly were in alignment with Herod's character and past behavior. Herod is *the* villain in our Advent story. Beyond the grief and sorrow of the story, Matthew was making a point. There is a clear parallel between Herod and past power players who oppressed God's people, power players like Pharaoh.

In the Book of Exodus, God's people found themselves enslaved to the whims and wishes of Pharaoh. He too was a powerful and paranoid ruler. Pharaoh oppressed God's people, but their oppression led to multiplication. They kept birthing new generations, and that multiplication fueled the Pharaoh's fear. Pharaoh determined that God's people had to be stopped.

Pharaoh tried to enlist the help of two Hebrew midwives, Shiphrah and Puah. Pharaoh also majored in manipulation. But Shiphrah and Puah, like the magi, resisted the manipulation. They came up with excuses as to why they could not destroy the Hebrew baby boys. And when Shiphrah and Puah brilliantly refused to do his bidding, Pharaoh took matters into his own hands. He ordered that every single baby boy born to a Hebrew family be thrown into the Nile River.

The story was the same story, but different power players. It was the same pattern, but different centuries. Theirs was the same political power and privilege but different dynasties. God has been doing the work of delivering people from oppression from the beginning. God has no fear of standing up against the powers of the day.

As the wind was whipping around me at Masada, I felt powerful standing on the top. And to imagine inhabiting a palace on what seemed to be the edge of the world, I could feel the seduction of that power seeping into my soul.

A Herod in Us All

I used to have this practice of giving some of my classmates nicknames in middle school. I would love to say that they were thoughtful, encouraging, and maybe winsome, but these names were not. The nicknames were mean, just plain old mean. I remember one time giving an unkind nickname to a girl in seventh-grade math class. I even made signs to place on the back of her chair, and yes, even a little jingle to go with my cruelty. I wanted to believe she liked the attention. I wanted to think that with all eyes on her, she felt seen.

But I know that was not true. I had the illusion that I was being funny, but my bullying was not funny. I believed the lie that bullying another human being would make me feel better. But bullying someone does not make us feel better. If anything, bullying destroys the bully from the inside and their target from the outside. Middle school is rough.

And yet what do Herod and I, and possibly you, have in common?

And yet what do Herod and I, and possibly you, have in common? Perhaps there have been moments in your life, middle-school moments, maybe yesterday moments, when you treated another human being as less than human. Maybe you let the Herod within guide your decisions, your choices, and your behaviors. Perhaps it's that moment when you decided just to lay right into the gossip of the day. Or maybe it's the moment when you destroyed a coworker in an argument because you had the upper hand or used your position in the company to gain power over other employees. It's the moment when you posted that embarrassing picture of your ex on Instagram or when you decided to get revenge by doing to someone what they clearly did to you.

We want to be right. We want to feel good. We want to justify ourselves. We want to win, and yes, sometimes at all costs. But other God-created human beings become the collateral damage in our rise to the top. We can destroy the humans around us. We become the Herods to their hurts, the Pharaohs to their pain, the villains in their stories and our own. It does not take long to become the villain.

> ## We become the Herods to their hurts, the Pharaohs to their pain, the villains in their stories and our own.

Villains shape our stories. Even when we have a solid sense of self, sometimes all it takes is one negative word and we are toast. Many of us remember moments in our lives when someone has spoken a negative word over us. With that negative word, they limit our potential and our power. Sometimes people don't even mean to, but like my middle-school self we give someone a name or a label and it shapes the view they have of themselves for years to come.

I call those negative words a "limitation prophecy." We speak negative words into someone's sense of self and it does some serious damage. So when someone places a limitation prophecy in our mind, we can become paralyzed and begin to embody that idea. It can happen to the best of us. It reminds me of the story of the prophet Elijah. Elijah had what we church-types call "a mountaintop experience."

Elijah traveled to Mount Carmel to face off with the prophets of Baal. He set up a test of sorts, an altar with a bull ready for sacrifice. There was just one catch, only a true god could light the fire. Elijah wanted to play fair, so he asked the prophets of Baal to go first. Minutes pass, then hours, and the prophets of Baal spent the day calling out to their god. The scene almost seemed comical; they are shouting, begging and even go as far as to ritually cut themselves and still no answer from Baal.

Elijah did not miss an opportunity to talk smack. Maybe your god is sleeping or traveling or going to the bathroom, Elijah taunted. But there was still no answer. And then came Elijah's turn. After soaking the altar with loads of water, Elijah prayed for God to show up. Fire from heaven burnt up the sacrifice, the altar, the water, and everything that surrounded it. God had won, so to speak, and Elijah was pumped. This hero-prophet of God defeated 450 false prophets of Baal. It's an epic Old Testament story of God blowing the competition away. One prophet of God versus 450 prophets of a mere idol!

One would think that Elijah would be excited, ready to conquer the world. He was high-fiving everyone around him. But all it took was one negative word. One limitation prophecy, and Elijah was ready to run.

After winning the battle, Elijah destroyed all 450 prophets of Baal. And not only did King Ahaz hear about it, but so did his wife, Queen Jezebel. She was not happy. She wanted to send Elijah a message: "May the gods deal with me, be it ever so severely, if by this time tomorrow I do not make your life like that of one of them" (1 Kings 19:2). What is a mere threat to a man who just defeated 450 prophets of Baal?

But Elijah was filled with fear and ran for his life. He ran with his servant all the way to Beersheba, the edge of the Northern Kingdom of Israel. And when he did not believe that was far enough, he ditched his servant and kept running into the wilderness where he was ready to give up and die. Elijah called out in exasperation, "'I have had enough, LORD,' he said. 'Take my life; I am no better than my ancestors.' Then he lay down under the bush and fell asleep" (1 Kings 19:4-5).

Elijah had a big limitation prophecy spoken over his life. In fact, Queen Jezebel spoke an outright curse over Elijah. Even though Elijah defeated 450 false prophets of Baal, even though Elijah should be high-fiving God, one limitation prophecy by Jezebel and Elijah is ready to run for his life. Now to be fair, Jezebel had some teeth to her threat. She was soon to be instrumental in stealing a neighbor's vineyard and having that neighbor executed. Jezebel, like Pharaoh and Herod, loved to manipulate the people around her. Elijah had just destroyed 450 prophets—most likely Jezebel's personal prophets—so he knew that she would want to make good on her promise. Still, how in such a short period of time did Elijah go from the mountaintop to the fetal position under a tree?

Elijah's story is strangely comforting because it reminds us that words are powerful. Threats are real. It reminds us that bullying has a lasting effect on the people around us. But before we get too quick to point our fingers at others, let's remember, bullies come in all shapes and sizes: the Pharaohs, the Herods, the King Ahazs, and Queen Jezebels and sometimes you as well.

> ## We need fictional characters to help us process the villain that we experience within.

Look I get it, cancel culture tells us that everyone is either good or bad, right or wrong, you are a bully, or you are not. But we know that life is so much more complex than the dichotomies we create. We like our villains because they make us feel good about ourselves. We need fictional characters to help us process the villain that we experience within. We may want to paint others in our story with a villain-sized brush, but we also know our own stories. The choices we have already made and the choices we did not make, but could have.

We also know the circumstances we find ourselves in. With a few more nods to bad behavior, our stories could change, and the stories of the people around us could change. We are terribly human. I wrestle with the so-called villains in our Bible stories. I want to know the story behind the story. I want to dig deeper and know why. Why the hunger for power? Why the hurt? Why the harm?

Perhaps there is space for building empathy for the villains. Not to justify their violence, injustice, or pain, but rather to recognize just how powerful we human beings truly are. Our lives matter! Our actions matter! Our words matter! They have the power to build up and tear down. "The tongue has the power of life and death, and those who love it will eat its fruit" (Proverbs 18:21).

Could it be that simple? Hurt people hurt people. When we hold on to our hurts and wounds, they become weapons formed against the people we love. We speak into existence pain we did not plan to inflict. And ironically, limitation prophesies we speak over others, we speak to ourselves as well. They become the pain and anxiety we inflict on ourselves every day. I am not enough. I will not get this promotion. I should not even try. By our very words we limit the good within and replay old messages that hold us back.

Limitation prophesies are a strong force. And if we hold on to those negative words, those old messages, before long we are placing limitation prophesies on the people around us. We make fun of our friends. We criticize our children. We cut down our spouse with our words. We speak limits even over the people we love. Our words become our weapon of choice. And we harm those around us. Even when we don't intend to, we play the villain in someone's story. There is a villain inside every one of us.

I imagine that Herod himself was not always Herod the Great. He, like you and me, probably had several limitation prophesies spoken over him. Perhaps his father told him he would never be enough. Maybe his family constantly compared him to a more successful relative. Or maybe he was schooled in the dog-eat-dog mentality that only the strongest survive. Could it be that violent words were just the currency of the political and religious elite into which he was born? It's easy to judge Herod and his life on this side of history. But could we build empathy for a child who was raised to rise to the top?

Beyond Herod attempting to survive in the Roman system, I imagine there was a lot in his life that led Herod to believe the lie that the only way to win was to climb over humans in his fight to the top. His family, the way he was raised, his sphere of influencers, his immersion in a culture of power, all primed Herod to play the villain. Herod was trained to be Herod the Great: Herod, terrorizer of the people; Herod, a not-so-good person; Herod the villain.

Standing at Masada, I suddenly started wondering why. Why Herod? Why such an unlikely character in God's redemptive story? God, you could choose anyone. So why choose this guy? And then it hit me: God became flesh and blood and moved into the neighborhood even for the Herods of the world. Herod was not left out of God's unlikely Advent story. The villain played a part in God's story of healing, redeeming, and restoring the whole wide world. Jesus came to redeem even seemingly unredeemables like Herod. Sometimes I do not want that to be true. I want to know where the boundaries are in God's salvation history. Who in the story is definitely in, and who is definitely out of God's family?

The Scandal of Love

Sometimes even preacher types like me want to limit the boundaries of God's love: there's no way Herod could have been included in God's plan to redeem the whole world through Jesus. Anyone but Herod. It is tempting to look at every story, including this one, and determine the good from the bad. Who is right and who is wrong? Who is in and who is out? Who deserves God's love and, well, who does not? But that is dangerous territory. Because this unlikely story of Advent is a story of a God that includes men and women like Zechariah and Elizabeth, who fear they have been placed on the shelf. God includes magi, who by birth are outside the circle of God's people. God includes an unwed teenaged mother, Mary, and her partner, a fearful and hesitant stepfather, Joseph.

> It is tempting to look at every story, including this one, and determine the good from the bad. Who is right and who is wrong?

And God included Herod, the villain who represented the possibilities for God's plan of redemption. Before we think we have it all figured out, perhaps we should be reminded anew of the scandal of God's love. God's scandalous love embodied in Jesus on more than one occasion produced outrage. God's scandalous love seemed offensive to the religious elite. God's scandalous love dined with tax collectors and sinners. God's scandalous love was anointed by women of ill repute. God's scandalous love was touched by leprous untouchables. And here in the Advent story, God's scandalous love includes the likes of the political tyrant Herod.

We struggle with God's scandalous love embodied in Jesus. Maybe we are a bit skeptical at another man's unlikely story. Jesus approached Nicodemus, a religious elite. He was a Pharisee, and he was cautiously curious about this street-preaching miracle worker. His curiosity led Nicodemus to secure a meeting with Jesus at night. It's not clear why. Was he cautious about what the others might think? Was Jesus simply less busy, available to Nicodemus only at night?

Whatever the case, Nicodemus had questions, and Jesus had answers. I am not sure Jesus had the answers that Nicodemus was looking for. Nicodemus wanted to be a part of what God was doing. He did not seem to understand Jesus's role in God's story. He believed that Jesus could come from God, but what was God up to through this Jesus character? It seemed like everything was being redefined to Nicodemus. Perhaps he was looking for a thread of connection to the religious foundations he had already known.

All of what Nicodemus thought he knew was in question. Now he was not so sure anymore. And his job, his role, his function in the community was certainty, clarity, and precision to the law. Nicodemus was a religious professional. How could he not understand the scandal of God's love? Jesus reminded Nicodemus that God was birthing anew. And in the middle of their challenging conversation the Gospel writer described God's scandalous love: "For God so loved the world that he gave his one and only Son, that whoever believes in him shall not perish but have eternal life. For God did not send his Son into the world to condemn the world, but to save the world through him" (John 3:16-17).

Healing was what Jesus was proclaiming all along.

God wants to save the whole world through Jesus. The Greek word here for "to save" is less about a get-out-of-hell-free card and more about wholeness: the healing, redemption, and restoration of the whole creation. Healing was what Jesus was proclaiming all along. God's kingdom is coming from heaven to earth. There is mysterious confusion baked right into God's kingdom. Sometimes we want a clear picture and a clear definition. But God's kingdom is coming, and it's no longer Herod's Judea, Pharaoh's Egypt, or even Rome's empire. This kingdom is ruled by the scandal of God's love. A scandal that looks over all the world, seeing the Herod within all of us and inviting us into a new way to live, a new way to be human, a new way to see the world around us. God's love invites us to be born anew. And when we witness the transforming power of that scandalous love, it transforms all of us.

Real Life Herods

In the fall of 2022, Mike Pratt, a retired elder in my congregation, asked me to meet with the leaders of Kindway. Kindway is an organization committed to investing in the lives of those impacted by incarceration. Kindway has an incredible record of partnering with God to transform people's lives. It seems to be a real solution to real problems. Less than 1.5 percent of the men and women who have graduated from Kindway's EMBARK program return to prison. Less than 1.5 percent! This in Ohio, a state where the recidivism rate is over 32 percent.[4]

It is miraculous! And after talking with the leaders of Kindway, I was determined to have them speak to my church family. I witnessed the transformation of God's scandalous love, and I knew my people needed to hear about it. So I invited Stan Stever, one of the participants in the Kindway program, to share his story on a Sunday morning. I had heard a portion of Stan's story and believed he was a Herod of sorts, an enemy, a villain in someone else's story and maybe even his own.

I was surprised that Stan had a bit of an entourage when he arrived at the church. These people were men and women who were part of the Kindway ministry that Stan brought with him. One man was just days from prison release and one of his first activities on this journey to freedom was to come to my church.

I invited Stan and his friends to sit with me up front, and during my sermon I invited Stan forward to share his story. Stan recalled that he was the youngest of eight children. His parents were workaholics, and that left Stan and his siblings to fend for themselves. He too had limitation prophesies spoken over him and was heavily bullied in third grade. Those messages and limitations left Stan very angry.

At first that anger lead to minor trouble. "I started vandalizing and breaking stuff," Stan explained. But the anger escalated and in time so did the trouble. "I need you to know I wasn't born a murderer. I didn't wake up one day and decide to take someone's life. In 1987 I took someone's life. I would go to prison at the age of seventeen, and I would spend the next thirty-four years of my life incarcerated."

> ## You have just invited a murderer to share his story in your church. How would the church respond to this?

I did not know that bit of Stan's story. I knew he had spent a long time in prison. I knew what he did was not good, and yet I did not know he had killed somebody. In that moment I thought to myself, *oh Rachel, you have done it now!* You have just invited a murderer to share his story in your church. How would the church respond to this?

In that moment, I knew God had something to teach me about my own bias toward the incarcerated. Sometimes I also want to limit God's love to those I believe don't deserve it. And a murderer doesn't always make my list of deserving people. Stan was only seventeen years old when he was incarcerated in a maximum-security prison for adults. My heart just sank as I heard Stan share about the terror he experienced in prison. For years he lived in fear and that fear led him to join a prison gang. He felt like he had to fight for his life. Stan had to survive. Prison life was full of abuse: mental, physical, and sexual. And although Stan believed he was strong and could fight, he could not fight the many. So, he was determined to be on a team of sort, and he joined a prison gang, the Aryan Brotherhood.

It was not difficult for Stan to be accepted by the Brotherhood; he had blue eyes, red hair, and fair skin. His countenance alone made him a poster child for this white supremacist gang inside the walls of the prison. At first, Stan said it felt very natural for him to be part of this gang. The Aryan brothers were violent, and he was violent. They were angry, and he was angry. Inflicting pain on another person felt good to Stan. Stan lived the gang life for years. But in 1999 Stan had a spiritual awakening. As he told the congregation:

> My mom came to visit me. I was in the hole, which is solitary confinement. There's no human contact 24/7. You're locked in this little room, and my mom came to visit me and when you get visits, you have to go to the visiting room so I was put in an orange jumpsuit. They put a belly chain on me. And they put handcuffs on me. And that's how I went out to see my mom. It wasn't the first time she seen me like that, it probably wasn't the hundredth time she saw me like that. I was always in trouble. I walked up to her, she had a tear in her eye. It made me mad. I said, Why are you crying, Mom? They are never going to break me! I am good." But she said, "Stanley when are you going to grow up?" I'm thirty years old. I am one of the head leaders in the Aryan Brotherhood. I'm doing life in prison, and everybody respects me, I thought fear was respect. And I said, Mom what do you mean? She said you're doing the exact same thing you were doing when you were thirteen years old: you are rebelling against authority, you are fighting, you are doing drugs, you are drinking! What's different? It made me mad! It made my pride swell up! And then I went back that day to my solitary confinement and

the only thing I could think of that was different
now than when I was thirteen years old, was that I
was doing life in prison. That's the only difference:
that's the only difference: I was a thirteen-year-old
kid doing life in prison! And that was the first time
that God pricked my heart.

God led Stan to become part of a Kairos weekend, a gathering
of prison insiders to explore and grow in Christian faith and
practice. He did not want to go to Kairos and it was one of his
own Aryan brothers that persuaded Stan to attend this four-day
Christian retreat in prison. On Halloween, October 31, 1999, Stan
said yes to following Jesus. And one might think that everything
changed in that moment for Stan, but it did not. Stan remarked,
"I went from being a drunken, gangbanging, violent heathen into
being a drunken, gangbanging, and violent Christian!"

Stan did not know how to follow Jesus. He was not raised in a
family that attended church. He did not know how to pray or even
where to start reading a Bible. But soon God would send people
into Stan's life to help Stan grow closer to God. That's how grace
works. Grace is not magic. It's not that you and I are instantly
changed, but over time we receive the grace that becomes a
refiner's fire in our hearts, minds, souls, and hands. We experience
the sanctifying grace of Jesus, and we grow in grace.

Stan continued to be shaped by men who taught him to be
kind and to love those around him. His anger began to subside.
God's love was healing him from the inside out when he met
a fellow inmate named Lee Tolbert. Lee and Stan were fast
friends. Although they were different—Stan was white and Lee
was black—they were both the youngest of eight children, both
incarcerated at seventeen years of age, both had very similar life

stories. Their connection was so deep that Stan described it as the kind of kinship that men and women experience while serving in the military. When you are in a dire situation you have each other's back. Lee and Stan had each other's backs and spent years teaching Bible studies, encouraging men one on one, and leading Kairos prison retreats with other men in the prison.

In 2014, their relationship was deeper than ever when Lee was diagnosed with prostate cancer. Stan was not a nurse and had zero medical training, but he was determined to care for his friend. Stan wanted to be clear that the state does not have a good medical system for the incarcerated, so Lee had little hope for survival. Stan became Lee's caretaker.

> I would wake up at 5:30 in the morning every morning. I would go down and I would clean him up. I would get him dressed. I would take him wherever he needed, the doctors' appointments. In 2018 there would come a time that he had digressed a lot and I came down at 5:30 in the morning just like I did every other morning and he was still laying there. And he was in a lot of pain. His cell had bunk beds and so he rested his arms on the top bunk bed. And you know I got down on my knees and I was pulling his diaper down. I have water and my rags and I was cleaning them up; and it's an amazing thing, God's scandalous love, and I'm cleaning him up and I hear laughing. And I look up and I'm like, Lee what are you laughing about? He looked down at me and he said, "If your Aryan brothers could see you now!" We just laughed! That's who Lee was! That's what

God used to get rid of that racial bigotry that was within me! That bigotry that a lot of us deal with still today!

Kindway entered the picture in Stan and Lee's story by attempting to help Lee with medical care. Stan was married before he left prison to a Jesus-loving woman. Stan determined with his wife that they would legally adopt Lee as their own so that Lee would have a family. Stan and his wife promised Lee that he would never die alone. Stan took care of Lee in the prison until Lee's medical condition deteriorated and he was sent to the state hospital.

Stan knew that once Lee was transferred to the medical hospital, he would no longer have the privilege of caring for Lee. Although Stan's wife could visit, Stan would not be allowed to see his dying friend. When describing his friend he said, "The spirit of the Lord was very overwhelming on his life, and when he passed away, it was thirty days before he was to be released into freedom. But what the world knows as freedom, God knows as bondage." Stan himself was released from prison less than four years ago.

When Stan had finished his testimony, I invited him to come and serve Communion with our leaders and pray over people. This is my body broken for you. This is my blood shed for all of you, even the villains in the room. That day I witnessed this villain-turned-Jesus-follower pray with people who were struggling. Some I imagine were struggling with Stan's message. Other people were struggling with their own story. Still others were struggling with the villain within themselves. We witnessed the power of God's scandalous love firsthand. The power of forgiveness is baked into the bread and cup and the story of life transformed by love.

> ## The power of forgiveness is baked into the bread and cup and the story of life transformed by love.

There is a Herod within us all. And friends, that is the scandal of Gods' love. God became flesh and blood. Immanuel: God is with us on the plateaus of Masada and in the darkness of solitary confinement. God was present in a mother's questions, and a son's response. God is with us in the laborers who gift their weekends to men and women through prison ministries, and in a moment that leads to healing, redemption, and restoration. Stan's unlikely story reminds us that God redeems the Herod in us all.

Your Unlikely Story

Do you recognize the Herod within? You better believe people had questions about Stan, and about Herod. What do you mean that there is a Herod in us all? It's difficult particularly, when the story becomes personal, to recognize that God's grace and love are available to everyone. It's difficult when your own family story has been wrecked by someone else's crime. It is difficult when we have placed the Herods of this world in a box and wanted to throw away the key. It is difficult when we've been shaped more by the Marvel Universe than the God who hung the stars in the universe. It is our human tendency to want to label, categorize, or even reject the role of the villain in our stories. But what if?

What if the light only breaks through the crack in our own story? What if the struggle is a part of it all? What if the only path to restoration is through brokenness? What if we all could name the Herods within ourselves?

What is your story? Where have you played the villain? Perhaps it was in someone else's story. Do you realize your own need for God's grace and love? What would it look like if you truly believed in the God of grace? What would it mean for you to believe in a Christ who died for the Herods of the world? Would it mean giving room for the restoration of the Herods in your life? Belief is more than a mere intellectual assent to some good ideas. Belief is staring in the face of a murderer and realizing that Jesus died for Stan, for this Herod. He makes God's list even when he doesn't always make mine. Grace changes the way we live, the way we pray, who we love, and how we love ourselves.

> We need one another to help us to see the path of healing, hope, and humility that makes us all human.

Standing on Masada, overlooking what once was the edge of the Dead Sea, I realized life from this view could obscure the folks in the valley, and then it is difficult not to succumb to the Herods within. We need God, oh yes, but we need one another to help us to see the path of healing, hope, and humility that makes us all human.

3

A Curious People

Chapter 3
A CURIOUS PEOPLE

I am always bursting with joy during Advent season. Call it excitement or anticipation, Advent is my absolute favorite time of year. Together with joy we actively await the coming of the Christ of Christmas, then and now. The anticipation is baked into our culture. Christmas is packed into every morsel of our existence: from the grandiose display of decorations at the local big box store, to the twinkling lights that gleam down main street in every small town. Advent joy is in the air, and it even has a soundtrack. "O Come, O Come Emmanuel," God with us, coming to us, and not merely us, but joy to the world! Beyond the classics bound in the pages of our hymnals, there are songs of the season that bring with them a bit of awe, wonder, and curiosity, songs like "I'm Dreaming of a White Christmas."

Perhaps you live in places that rarely witness the fall of these bits of powdery perfection, but I happen to live in the Midwest. And snowfall brings with it a childlike awe and wonder for me. True confession: I cry each year when I see the first snow coming down from the sky. There is something majestic about it; the first snow feels like magic. Snow is basically cosmic magic. So, when I see that first snow, my heart swells and so does my curiosity.

We had such heavy snowfall in my childhood that we would create caverns through the snow drifts along the side of the road. We had to be careful because there was too much traffic and cars would stop to inform our parents that we were playing in snow too close to the road. We could play in the snow for hours and then unbundle for a little bit of hot chocolate. Soon we would head back into the cold until the sun quit shining.

It's like my childhood self was totally chill resistant. Cold resistant until someone pelted me in the face with a snowball and then I finally realized just how cruel those ice crystals could be. But it would take more than a snowball fight to keep me from playing in the snow. That first snow feels like a miracle, and I joyfully anticipate the winter weather in the season that follows. The Advent season brings with it a miraculous curiosity, in the songs that we sing, the food that we prepare, the snow that falls, the loved ones around the table, and the presents under the tree.

An Unlikely Gift

I'm not very materialistic when it comes to gifts and the giving of gifts. Although I really enjoy giving gifts, I have a ton of baggage around receiving gifts because my birthday is December 19. Most December babies I know have experiences where they received a birthday-slash-Christmas present. Or maybe even, "Sorry sweetness, there just was not the time and attention to plan a birthday party!" December birthdays can be tough. Christmas is just around the corner and so Jesus's birthday really does outplay mine. But a couple of years ago I received what may be the most meaningful gift I have ever received for my birthday.

I was part of a small group of women from Ginghamsburg Church. Each week we met together and talked about faith, family, food, and the Bible. We prayed together and served in the community together. The best way to describe our group is to say that we did life together. And so on this particular birthday my small group commissioned wall art from a local artist. The gift was a wood sign that would hang in my dining room.

My friend handed me this very heavy package. I wondered what it could be. As I peeled back the wrapping paper, I began to tear up. This wooden piece was painted white with black lettering that declared, "Because Jesus Eats with Everyone." The sign nearly took my breath away. I cried because it captured my heart and our mission as a family. It was a simple and yet profound gift that I could hang in my home. People would get it; people would get me.

My spouse, Jon, and I had a monthly practice that we called Open Table. We would open our home for a dinner every week and then eventually once a month. We invited everybody, and I do mean everybody, over for dinner. There were neighbors, friends, coworkers, family, church folks, and, yes, even strangers who found a place to belong in our home. The concept of Open Table was simple. Host a dinner where everyone contributes. We created a Facebook group, and we would post a menu: the Billups family is making tacos. We invited everybody to bring something to share.

In the seven and a half years we hosted Open Tables, we never ran out of food. There were times that it felt a bit like the young boy's lunch of two fish and five loaves in the Gospel of John. We would worry because we had twenty people who did not RSVP.

Would we have enough food? And in the middle of our worry, someone would show with six pizzas.

It was a multiplying miracle. We never ran out of food; there was always enough. We were not exactly sure how many people would show up each week. Sometimes twenty people would gather, and we would sit cozily around our large dining room table. The conversations were rich, intimate, and deep. At other times, one hundred people would show, and Jon and I would be setting up tables in the garage, on the back porch, in the living room, and anywhere we could find space. The energy was electrifying, and I would hop from table to table to ensure I said hello to everyone. There was always enough food and always room for more people.

We always wanted to extend the edges of our table to everybody. Each month suddenly our home became a place where very different people gathered to eat, to pray, and even to love. It felt like God's kingdom come, "on earth as it is in heaven." I never want to place boundaries on God's love or what God's love can do in and through unlikely human beings like you and me. And that wooden sign said it all, because Jesus eats with everyone.

> In the Advent season we have the most unlikely of gifts in the baby Jesus, God with us in the form of a newborn baby, tender, vulnerable, and terribly human.

Perhaps you have had something meaningful given to you: a gift handmade with love, a trip of a lifetime, a present that someone saved over the course of years. Whatever the gift was, the gift was more than a piece of material. It somehow captured your essence, your mission, who you want to be in the world. Just thinking about it brings tears to your eyes. In the Advent season we have the most unlikely of gifts in the baby Jesus, God with us in the form of a newborn baby, tender, vulnerable, and terribly human. And did you know that even the sweet baby Jesus received an unlikely gift from a curious people? This time it seems like God extended the edges of God's table to include an unlikely group of travelers in the Advent story.

The Holy Family opened their home—their table, if you will—for this group of outsiders bearing gifts. They were the magi. They traveled from the east. They were an unlikely group in search of something, well, really someone. They seemed to have influence, because when they came looking for a newborn king they stopped at Herod's palace and asked, "Where is the one who has been born king of the Jews? We saw his star when it rose and have come to worship him"(Matthew 2:2). These outsiders looked to the stars for direction, meaning, and purpose. Like my childhood self, they too experienced awe and wonder as they looked to the sky. What was happening with this star? Was this some supernova? Did the magi encounter an astronomical irregularity? Some scholars have attempted to match the appearance of the star to a historical astronomical occurrence, but it's possible Matthew was just alerting us to something very unique and special. These magi from the east, most likely Persian outsiders to the Jewish faith, would have had their own version of heavenly predictions.

What the magi saw in the sky compelled them to travel hundreds of miles, determined to pay a visit to the ruler of Judea, Herod the Great. For these magi, this cosmic irregularity signals something special, something divine. The star signaled a divine expectation. Could it be that these curious travelers would encounter something that would change the whole world? Could this give them the meaning and the purpose that they had been longing for? Would this star help them to understand their place in the world?

Yes, the magi had been looking at the sky with mysterious curiosity, but this time instead of snow, they were peering at an unusual star. The star captured their curiosity so much so that they would risk visiting a ruler with such a violent reputation. They had questions and the courage to ask. So, the magi asked Herod, "Where is this king of the Jews?" Awkward, because Herod believed that King of the Jews was his title, his function, his position, and his power.

The magi's very presence set Herod on edge, and Herod consulted the religious experts around him and asked where the Messiah was to be born:

> *"In Bethlehem in Judea," they replied, "for this is what the prophet has written:*
>
> > *'But you, Bethlehem, in the land of Judah,*
> > *are by no means least among the rulers of Judah;*
> > *for out of you will come a ruler*
> > *who will shepherd my people Israel.'"*
>
> (Matthew 2:5-6)

The magi traveled to the little town of Bethlehem to greet the child and his family. They carried with them Herod's request to return to Herod with the child's location. Herod was making a political move. He depended on the magi to follow through with his request. Matthew does not fill in the gap between Jerusalem and Bethlehem. We do not know what the magi were thinking.

The reader was not even given the contents of their conversation or their first impression of the Judean ruler. Would the magi turn out to be political allies with Herod? Would they see past his pseudo honor and curiosity? And there was Herod's reputation. Did they know or at the very least discern his anger and violent tendencies?

Herod and all of Jerusalem were already "greatly disturbed" by the magi. I imagine the magi noticed the awkward stares and the looks of mistrust. They were outsiders and treated as such. Herod may have been the villain, but the magi were the outsiders. Humans tend to prefer the villain they know over the outsider they don't know. In this atmosphere of political tension, baby Jesus received a very unlikely gift. After Herod gave the magi a general description of where to find the baby, they looked to the star for further guidance. They were overjoyed with what they saw. The star hovering above a household. How could the magi be sure? Was this the house? Was this the child? Matthew tells us, "On coming to the house, they saw the child with his mother Mary, and they bowed down and worshiped him. Then they opened their treasures and presented him with gifts of gold, frankincense and myrrh" (Matthew 2:11).

The magi offered Jesus an unlikely gift: three of them, actually. They presented Jesus with gold, frankincense, and myrrh. It's unclear why these specific gifts. The gifts would have been expensive gifts and originated in countries to the east of Judea. Some scholars imagine them to be forms of incense with powerful scents. These gifts evoke curiosity and mystery. Why these specific gifts? Early church fathers like Epiphanius believed that the gifts were a foreshadowing of Jesus's life, death, and resurrection: the gold represented Jesus's humanity, the frankincense Jesus's divinity, and the myrrh his death.[1] These gifts do seem to be inspired by references from the Old Testament. The writer of Matthew was intentional to connect those dots, first from the prophet Isaiah and then with the psalm:

> *Herds of camels will cover your land, young camels of Midian and Ephah. And all from Sheba will come, bearing gold and incense and proclaiming the praise of the* LORD.
>
> Isaiah 60:6

And also perhaps, in the poetry of the psalmist:

> *May the kings of Tarshish and of distant shores bring tribute to him. May the kings of Sheba and Seba present him gifts. May all kings bow down to him and all nations serve him.*
>
> Psalm 72:10-11

These were gifts fit for a king. But why would these magi bring gifts to a baby? It seems that the gifts could have been more practical. Gold, frankincense, and myrrh seem like luxury for a family in need of baby wipes and diapers. With my first child, I recall having a conversation with a woman who insisted I invest in a wipe warmer for our soon-to-be-newborn. I knew enough to know enough. I knew that a wipe warmer was an added step in the diapering process that I was convinced I would not use. I thought that was a bit much.

> ## These were gifts fit for a king. But why would these magi bring gifts to a baby?

What is the child Jesus going to do with gold, frankincense, and myrrh? Perhaps these gifts give us more insight about the givers, rather than the gifts themselves. These are unlikely gifts, presented in a peculiar place.

A Peculiar Place

The magi find Jesus in Bethlehem of Judea. Bethlehem was basically a suburb of the city of Jerusalem. Jerusalem at the time of Jesus's birth would have only touted one hundred thousand people and Bethlehem a fraction of that population. Bethlehem was a town of shepherds. Sheep were in high demand for the running of the religious machine in the Temple in Jerusalem. Bethlehem was a great place to find sheep, but not exactly prime real estate.

Why choose Bethlehem as the birthplace of the coming Messiah? The Gospel of Matthew tells us: "When he [Herod] had called together all the people's chief priests and teachers of the law, he asked them where the Messiah was to be born. 'In Bethlehem in Judea,' they replied" (Matthew 2:4-5a).

Bethlehem was associated with Israel's championed King David. The prophet Samuel anointed David king in Bethlehem and David laid claim to its boundaries as his home. Throughout the Old Testament and through the time of Jesus, Bethlehem's population remained small, a mere village. There certainly were connections made between Bethlehem and the Old Testament prophets' messianic predictions. Although some scholars contend that the messianic connection to Jesus is an invention of the Gospel writers themselves, others believe that Bethlehem as the birthplace of Jesus would have been an embarrassment to those first Jesus followers.[2] Bethlehem as a birthplace has its share of controversy.

But what about those Old Testament connections? The author of Matthew seems to be referencing the prophet Micah who declared, "But you, Bethlehem Ephrathah, though you are small among the clans of Judah, out of you will come for me one who will be ruler over Israel, whose origins are from of old, from ancient times" (Micah 5:2).

The prophet warned God's people that they would be in exile until the woman gave birth to a son and the rest of his family returned to join the remnant in Israel. Micah embraced a messiah as shepherd of God's people: "He will stand and shepherd his flock in the strength of the LORD, in the majesty of the name of the LORD his God. And they will live securely, for then his greatness will reach to the ends of the earth" (Micah 5:4).

Micah functioned as the mouthpiece of God giving the people a prophetic promise. Sometimes when we think of prophecy we may think of Nostradamus, fortune telling, or even folks who say really mean things just to scar and scare people. But that was not God's purpose for the prophet. Prophets like Micah were used by God to bring a word of hope and healing to God's people, even when that word of hope came with a warning.

We understand that Micah was speaking to a particular group of people at a particular time. This prophetic word was meant to be a word of hope to God's people as the people experienced oppression from an outside source. Certainly, that would have sounded familiar to the people living in Bethlehem at the time of the birth of Jesus. God's people knew occupation, they understood oppression. They longed for hope and healing. In Micah's day, those oppressors could have been the Assyrians or even the Babylonians. These outside groups really messed up God's people.

But prophetic promises have more than one function. As followers of Jesus, we read Micah through a different lens. This was a word of hope to God's people, but this hope has future implications. We read Micah chapter 5 through the lens of the good news of the gospel of Jesus. Matthew was connecting the dots from Micah's promise to Jesus's birthplace. Perhaps it's a bit clearer in the Message paraphrase: "They told him, 'Bethlehem, Judah territory. The prophet Micah wrote it plainly: It's you, Bethlehem, in Judah's land, no longer bringing up the rear. From you will come the leader who will shepherd-rule my people, my Israel'" (Matthew 2:6 MSG).

> **Perhaps you have had a similar experience. The place where you grew up, the town that you call home may also be a peculiar place.**

Matthew declared: we have heard this story before. God has given this peculiar place meaning and purpose. Bethlehem was a contrast to the power and prestige of Jerusalem. And certainly, a contrast to the power and privilege of Rome. I wonder if Herod even had much interest in Bethlehem. Without the visit of the magi, without this threat to his power, would Herod have given Bethlehem a second thought? Out of Bethlehem, from this small seemingly insignificant place comes the Messiah, the Anointed One, the Savior of the world. Just because Bethlehem is a seemingly small place does not mean it deserves a bad reputation. Perhaps you have had a similar experience. The place where you grew up, the town that you call home may also be a peculiar place.

I will never forget sitting in eighth-grade social studies class. One of my classmates discovered I was from the booming metropolis of Laurelville, Ohio. Truth was that I grew up ten miles outside of even that town of seven hundred people. My peer announced, "Rachel, there is no way you are from Laurelville. You are too smart to be from Laurelville."

He had an assumption that certain people live in certain places. That anyone who was raised in such a thin slice of life could not be intelligent. He was wrong, not only about me, but also about many people that I knew and loved from Laurelville. Smart, dare I say brilliant, people lived there. How do you respond to criticisms of your peculiar place? Whether it was because of the location of your elementary school, what side of town you grew up on, or even the fact that your mail was delivered to a particular zip code, people had assumptions about you, your family, and your origins. They could not imagine anything amazing and brilliant coming from such a place.

Perhaps you live in a peculiar place, and you find yourself defending your spot on the earth. I have encountered so many people in ministry who have let the place they grew up determine their destiny. Remember that God uses what God chooses. This kind of conversation should signal to us a spiritual red flag. People love to limit people with their words. But God specializes in using limited spaces for God's extraordinary work. Throughout Scripture, God seems to do concentrated work in peculiar places.

> Bethlehem is this unlikely, insignificant place for God to become flesh and blood and move into the neighborhood.

Bethlehem is this unlikely, insignificant place for God to become flesh and blood and move into the neighborhood. And yet when God chooses Bethlehem, it's so in alignment with the contrast between God's redeeming and restoring work and the destruction of the political players of the day. God has a way of turning our assumptions on their heads. Bethlehem became the birthplace of the Messiah. So, Jesus has received an unlikely gift, in an equally peculiar place.

A Curious People

Numerous Nativity scenes place the magi alongside Mary, Joseph, and baby Jesus, and often the shepherds as well. Nearly always three magi, even though Scripture never tells the number of Magi visiting the Holy Family and Bethlehem. Perhaps people were making connections between the magi and the gifts: three gifts, therefore three magi. Some scholars believe the "three magi" represented merely the leadership or presenters of those gifts. They speculated that an entire group traveled together. Church tradition has even given these magi names and at times called them kings: Caspar, Balthasar, Melchior.

Placing the magi in the Nativity scene was not exactly chronologically accurate. It was doubtful that the magi visited a newborn Jesus. For starters Matthew does not describe the setting as a stable, but rather "the home" where Mary, Joseph, and Jesus were staying. There is no mention of the manger or even a borrowed space. Ownership was unclear; perhaps Mary, Joseph, and Jesus were living with relatives in Bethlehem for an extended stay. Could this be a family home? And if it was a family home, why not use the home for Jesus's birth?

In any event, time seemingly passed, so when King Herod realized the magi did not return to Jerusalem, he ordered the slaughter of boys two years old and younger. Herod wanted to eliminate the threat, cover his bases, and know the whole of the timeline and travel itinerary of the magi. He did not want even a toddler to take his place as king of Judea.

Most likely the magi were visiting a toddler Jesus.

Most likely the magi were visiting a toddler Jesus. Perhaps you have witnessed a toddler receiving gifts? As a momma, I can only imagine Jesus responding excitedly to these new gifts. There would be almost no response from a newborn baby when receiving a gift, or even a one-year-old child, but there is something joyful that happens when your child becomes eighteen months old—and Christmas with a two-year-old is sheer delight. I recognize that many two-year-olds find more joy in tearing the wrapping paper than the gift itself. But I cherish the awe and wonder in the eyes of a toddler when he or she receives a gift.

Imagine a two-year-old Jesus discovering something as shiny and colorful as gold. Perhaps Jesus was shy and holding on to his mother as these strangers step into his home. And they are not deterred by the humble surroundings of a poor family in Bethlehem. Perhaps the humility of the situation confirmed their cosmic suspicion. This must be divine destiny. God's surprise added to their awe and wonder. Is there something about the child Jesus that enhanced their curiosity? How about your curiosity?

Some children seem to have a spiritual curiosity embedded in their personality. Several years ago, I met a toddler girl who served as a greeter at church with her grandmother. People gave her the name "angel child." There was something about her attention to people and her love for all things worship that seemed well beyond her years and perhaps even holy. I welcomed her joyful face nearly every weekend.

Then one weekend she became sick, and the sickness quickly spread into her brain. Although the family and I clung to the hope that she would battle through, this precious child did not make it. And her sudden passing left a mark on the hearts, minds, and experiences of many who attended church. "She was an angel," some remarked. Perhaps you have known a child that seemed to have a sensitivity to all things spiritual.

What kind of Christ child did the magi experience?

Was Jesus that kind of toddler? What kind of Christ child did the magi experience? And when the magi presented Jesus with gifts of gold, frankincense, and myrrh, how did the toddler Jesus respond? Was he wide-eyed with awe and wonder? Or was he peering around the leg of his mother or father? Could he have been so surprised that Jesus acted out in front of these foreign magi?

And these magi were not exactly kings. History has a couple of descriptors for magi, either Persian fire gods or astrologers.[3] The Greek word for *magi*, "magos," can mean wise men, astrologers, priests, but also magician or sorcerers as well.[4] Some scholars connect the magi to the Zoroastrian tradition. The magi are a bit odd. At first glance, they seem like pagan performers, outside of the people of God. If they are fire priests, they are certainly too in tune with the earth to be considered in the narrow definition of the people of God at the time.

75

I cannot help but think of the magi as performing sacred rituals and maybe—just maybe—a walk over hot coals or a fire-breather in their midst. But whether priests, magicians, or sorcerers, they are certainly paying attention to the stars. The Old Testament is not exactly kind to the folks in these categories: "Do not turn to mediums or seek out spiritists, for you will be defiled by them. I am the LORD your God" (Leviticus 19:31).

These magi are not religious insiders. They are not church peeps. The magi have no political power in Judea, and they certainly do not have religious ties to the people. The magi are outsiders. At the time of Jesus's birth, the religious elites did not appear to understand what God was doing. The most powerful of them reject Jesus as a threat. And it was these stargazing fire priests, the curious ones, the unlikely ones, who come to worship Immanuel, God with us. When they see Jesus and his mother Mary, the magi bow down in humble worship. They made an offering of gifts to this child. They share their very best in joyful anticipation of the future.

> The magi have no political power in Judea, and they certainly do not have religious ties to the people.

How do they know to worship Jesus? How can they already understand his divine purpose? As though it's not shocking enough that these fire priests worship the Jesus the religious elite will refuse to listen to, they hear a warning in a dream not to go back to Herod the Great. The magi obey the warning and return home by another route.

But who warns the magi? Does God warn these religious outsiders? How do the magi both understand the implications of this toddler Jesus and attend to the voice of God warning them in a dream? Could it be that right here in the Christmas story God is challenging our assumptions, messing with our definitions of whom God chooses and uses for God's purposes? Never put boundaries around the places God chooses, the people God uses, and what God chooses to do. Our boundaries keep people out, and on our worst days they discourage folks from coming close to the Savior.

It is heartbreaking to experience the religious obstacles that followers of Jesus place in front of so-called outsiders to keep them from experiencing Jesus. Serious question: If we were the ones writing God's story, would we have given the magi a front-row seat to God's salvation? Do we celebrate those outside our faith tradition who sometimes seem to understand God's bigger picture better than those of us who consider ourselves religious insiders? In our quest to be right, have we lost our ability to look to the sky with curiosity and joy? Have we mistakenly uninvited whole groups from God's table?

Have you ever had an experience of being uninvited? Perhaps you never made the guest list. I remember in middle school being asked to leave a lunchroom table because I did not exactly make the cut. Middle school seems like practice in attempting to figure out your place in this world. I attended a middle school where four elementary schools converged to combine into one junior high school. It was not surprising that the connections I had made in elementary school were severed by classes, schedules, and extracurricular activities.

I was a bit desperate to find my people. I wanted a place to belong. On that first day of seventh grade, I spotted a table of athletes. These were girls I knew from summer camps and basketball practice. Some would grow up to become future teammates, but at the time our interests were still uncertain. Besides these athletes were pretty cool. Perhaps I was too zealous in my determination to be with the cool kids that I miscalculated my own cool factor.

One random day, I was asked to move to another table: "We think you would be more comfortable at another table, Rachel. There are just too many people around this one." Truthfully, the table was getting a little crowded and so they certainly had a practical point. But their ask was painful. I moved to a new table and made new connections with a new group of friends. But the feeling of being uninvited is hard to expel from your head and your heart.

What about you? Being uninvited does not merely happen in the cafeteria. It's the moment you are not invited to the friend's party, the family gathering, or the work trip. These tables represent inclusion, love, and even promotion, and yet to be told you do not belong can be devastating. I imagine many of us have stories where we have been uninvited. Perhaps reading these words even pricks your heart a bit. But also imagine that sometimes we have been the ones to exclude others. Sometimes we are the ones uninviting others from our table.

Have you accidently kept someone out of God's story? With your words, have you attempted to eliminate whole groups of people from God's plan? Are there people you have been crossing off God's list? Certain people are in, and certain people are out?

Ultimately the magi remind us of the inclusive umbrella of the gospel. The good news that Jesus became flesh and blood and moved into the neighborhood. Yes, God was one of us! Even the Christmas story turns our definitions of power and privilege upside down and inside out. The powerful are left wondering, the religious scratching their heads, the biggest cities and brightest places are seemingly passed by, and the outsider is earning the lead role in God's unfolding story of hope and healing for the world. Did you know that the magi were an integral part of God's story? Did you know this has been God's plan all along?

A couple of years ago, I found myself wondering what to do. It was in a moment when hurt and harm had been done to our LGBTQ+ siblings. Perhaps you too experienced this moment. I knew I could not be quiet. And like many others I went to social media to express my grief. I did not turn to social media to keep people out, but rather I turned to social media to invite people in.

I was reminded of the words of Jesus's traveling companions on the road to Emmaus. After the resurrection, Cleopas and his traveling companion were walking together. Jesus decided to join them on their journey. For whatever reason they did not recognize Jesus. Jesus asked a few simple questions that led Cleopas to spill his grief on the listening stranger. He criticized Jesus for being the only visitor in Jerusalem who didn't know what was happening with Jesus of Nazareth. It was all over Facebook—well, sort of.

This Jesus character was a prophet. He performed so many miracles before God and everyone. And he made the religious elites pretty nervous. So nervous in fact that they handed him over to Rome for a death sentence and real-life execution. Man, how do you not know what has been going on for these last few days in Jerusalem? Cleopas, overcome with his own grief, declared, "But we had hoped that he was the one who was going to redeem Israel. And what is more, it is the third day since all this took place" (Luke 24:21).

Cleopas had lost hope. Three days meant no hope for Jesus's survival. Jesus was dead and so were Cleopas's dreams for the future. I so identified with the grieving Cleopas. I felt like my dreams for the future were lost and I too was grieving. So, I posted an invitation to gather for Open Table.

> Jesus is present as we walk together in this journey. Jesus is present as we show each other signs of hospitality and love. Jesus is present at the table.

I had hoped that we would have embraced our Wesleyan heritage to do no harm. I had hoped that I would not have witnessed the countless LGBTQ+ persons hurting, grieving, and asking the question, *Am I really welcome in the church?* I had hoped we would have given our culture, our world a new paradigm that says unity is not uniformity. I had hoped to post something different. But much like the two traveling on the road to Emmaus, I am reminded that Jesus is present even when I cannot recognize him. Jesus is present as we walk together in this journey. Jesus is present as we show each other signs of hospitality and love. Jesus is present at the table.

I did not know what else to do but to open a table. The invitation went out: that's right, the Billups are hosting Open Table this Friday night. It's simple. We will share dinner together. Just bring a dish to share. All—and I mean all—are welcome to come eat together, pray together, and love one another. If you need my address, send me a message. You are invited!

The next Sunday a person approached me and asked if he was truly invited to my home for this gathering. He was known for harshly sharing his opinions in and outside of the church when it came to the inclusion of our LGBTQ+ siblings. To be honest, at first, I froze. I wanted to say no, you are not invited! I wanted to protect the people that I love.

And then in a moment that felt like the nudge of the Holy Spirit, I heard God whisper, "Jesus eats with everyone." Dag it! Jesus does eat with everyone. Jesus found himself at tables with strangers, critics, and many folks who did not agree in theology or practice. And so I said, "Yes, you are welcome to come. You are welcome to come to grieve with those who grieve and to love on your siblings who need care and attention. But if you are determined to cause harm, please do not come." He smiled and thanked me for my invitation and then did not show up for the Open Table.

And truthfully, I was not disappointed that he was a no-show. Because love and harm cannot coexist. There is no room for harm in love. So, that night we had a party to celebrate that everyone is a beloved child of God. Jesus eats with everyone. Jesus had a thing for hospitality. He got himself invited to the best parties and he did not give a lick about what his skeptics might have thought about his table manners. Jesus eats with everybody!

The magi signal to us that opening God's home and God's table was God's plan all along. Everyone is welcome to come and worship the Christ with joyful curiosity. I love that the magi mess with our definitions of inclusion. They bend our understanding of the people of God. Together we have experienced an unlikely gift, in a peculiar place, presented by a curious people, so that ordinary folks like you and me can experience an unprecedented, undeserved, unexpected, unlikely Advent.

Your Unlikely Story

Perhaps you have nearly crossed church off your list, or maybe you know and love someone who has left church behind. They have been turned off by religious types. They have come to believe that church is not the place for them. And yet this story, God's story of using the most curious of people, the magi, for God's purposes, reminds us that God does not draw small circles. God does not cross guests off the list. God extends God's arms of love into places and spaces that mess with our definitions of love: the inclusive umbrella of the gospel.

Everyone is part of God's bigger story, God's plan of healing and restoring the whole wide world. Real talk: When you think about extending the edges of your table, or when you decide to extend an invitation to the stranger, does it bring you anxiety? Does it nearly take your breath away? I get it; not all of us are extroverts. Beyond our personality types, would you rather God draw a small circle or are you ready for God's love to be deep and wide?

During the season of Advent, I prayerfully ask God to open my mind and heart to people who need an invitation. Sometimes it's into my home for a meal, and other times into the church for God's table. I pray that God would place a person on my heart and in my mind who is in need of a bit of joy this season. Who could use a little awe and wonder?

Some years I make a list. Some people I invite to participate online because they live far away from the church I am serving. Still others I ask to come and experience the worship during Advent or even on Christmas Eve. I promise to save them a seat, meet them at the door, and I ask our greeters to ensure everyone feels welcome.

Over the years, I have witnessed friends and family drive hours to experience the joy of Christmas Eve. I have witnessed Christmas Eve become a spiritual catalyst in people's lives. Perhaps it is time for you to extend an invitation to a friend, a family member, or a coworker who needs to experience an unlikely Christmas. Not a Christmas where they will feel beat up for their questions or skepticism. People do not need a Christmas where they have to get all their stuff together. Christmas was never meant for people to feel like religious outsiders. Rather it is meant for people to experience an unlikely Christmas where the table is open, extra chairs are pulled up, and we are all living this truth: Jesus eats with everybody.

4

When God
Shows Up

4

Chapter 4
WHEN GOD SHOWS UP

I have always felt drawn to the shepherds. Maybe it's because I grew up on a family farm. And although we did not raise sheep, there were cattle, chickens, and the occasional pig to raise. My affinity for the shepherds is that they are regular people, unlikely to experience a divine encounter in the middle of their late-night work shift. If this is true for the shepherds, then perhaps you and I could experience God in the middle of our ordinary lives. I invite you to open your eyes to the unlikely moments in your regular life where God is already present, already showing up. If you are anything like me there's a lot of holiday busyness to weed through in order to stop long enough to see God in the middle of an unlikely day.

But I desperately need God's presence and peace. Each year at the onset of the Advent season, I need a fresh dose of Jesus in my life. In order to experience the Christ of Christmas, I have to set my intention. If not, it seems that overnight I get caught up in the busyness of the Advent season. And I do it to myself. I overplan and underestimate the time my family and I will need to make it through all the planning and preparation that fills our calendar until Christmas Day.

Instead of decking the halls, I find myself herding cats. Advent sometimes feels like preparing for the most wonderfully chaotic time of the year. I struggle to be at peace. Advent is a season where we actively wait for the Christ of Christmas, and yet waiting is not always easy. In a season that can be hijacked by the consumerism of our day, it is difficult not to get caught up in the frenzy to buy more, do more, and celebrate more. Our lives and calendars are bursting with activity. We feel hurried, but we sanctify the chaos with a casual "it's the season."

But can we just agree that the Advent season comes at the same time, year after year, every year? Christmas Eve is always on December 24 and Christmas Day is always December 25, and yet some of us find ourselves scrabbling. It's as if we are surprised. We are in a rush to make plans with friends and family. We speed to drive the kids to Christmas play practice or to rush to the completion of this year's choral Christmas cantata. There are greens to be hung, songs to be sung, lines to be learned, and gifts to be given away.

I always say an extra prayer for the present procrastinators, those of you who wait until Christmas Eve to make a list, let alone check it twice. It is a risk to wait until the last minute. Here in the Midwest, you never know what the weather is going to bring you. It can be a balmy fifty degrees in the days leading up to Christmas, but there are years where the snow piles up or the temperatures plummet.

But whether your holiday stress is self-imposed or merely the circumstances you find yourself in, you feel hurried and anxious. Most of us long for a bit of holiday peace. We want breathing space. We long for space to savor the season. Is there time to soak it all in? What could it look like to embrace with awe and with gratitude the present moment of grace? When you try to sanctify chaos, it doesn't work, because God had been sanctifying it all along. Sanctification is God's job! I will let you in on some insider information: even pastor types talk a great game at the beginning Advent. We say to ourselves, "This year is going to be different. This is my year to keep a reasonable pace. This Advent season I will live the unforced rhythms of grace."

Most of us long for a bit of holiday peace.

And then we come to a point in the season where actively waiting seems impossible. We get caught up in the frenzy of human *doing* rather than the peace of human *being*. We throw up our hands and perhaps even a prayer that shouts, God, just help me survive! Maybe you are having a moment where the Advent season seems more like a sprint to the finish line rather than an opportunity to be shaped by the Prince of Peace.

This is why I believe that gathering for worship during the season of Advent is so vital. Whether you are gathering from your kitchen table at home or sitting next to your bestie at church, intentional worship has potential to reorient our lives. We are a forgetful people, and our calendars need a regular reminder that a life-giving pace is possible. Worship can help us to reset our rhythms and remind us of Jesus's invitation in Matthew that Eugene Peterson so beautifully captured in his paraphrase:

Are you tired? Worn out? Burned out on religion? Come to me.
Get away with me and you'll recover your life. I'll show you
how to take a real rest. Walk with me and work with me—
watch how I do it. Learn the unforced rhythms of grace. I won't
lay anything heavy or ill-fitting on you. Keep company with me
and you'll learn to live freely and lightly.

Matthew 11:28-29, MSG

I imagine we gather together for worship for a variety of reasons. For some there is a nostalgia for worship during Advent: the music, the smells, the lighting of the Advent wreath. Worship feels like a warm cup of milk that you are longing to sip, and Advent does not feel like Advent until you sing the songs of your childhood. For others, Advent worship is merely part of what you do. It is like exercise or even taking your daily multivitamin. It is what keeps you spiritually healthy.

> Whatever the case, many of us long
> for peace. We want to experience
> a real rest. We want to have an
> encounter with the divine.

For others, you are just dipping your toe into this season we call Advent. Perhaps Advent seems a little strange. You are fairly new to this church stuff and you long for a new way to be human. Of course, you are familiar with all things Christmas, but four weeks of preparation and actively waiting for Jesus to come is brand-new to you. Whatever the case, many of us long for peace. We want to experience a real rest. We want to have an encounter with the divine.

Looking for a Sign

No matter why you are gathering for worship, I think it is safe to say that most of us have questions, hopes, longings, and dreams for our lives. We long for confirmation that we are moving in the right direction. We humans want to know we are getting life right. We desire peace: peace of mind, peace in our schedules, peace that directs our path. And when you do not know where to go or where to find peace, sometimes you discover you are whispering under your breath, Just give me a sign!

> When certainty evades our minds and our hearts, when peace seems like a distant memory and the only constant is desperation, we want a sign. And that is what we find the shepherds receiving in the Christmas story.

We want signs. We long for guideposts along life's journey to reassure us that we are not messing up. Sometimes we want a simple sign so that we can take the next step. Make it easy for me, God! But other times it is much more complicated than a simple sign. When our dreams and longings are big: like a shift in career, a move across the country, a medical plan, a college major, or even a change in relationship status, we are desperate for a sign. When certainty evades our minds and our hearts, when peace seems like a distant memory and the only constant is desperation, we want a sign. And that is what we find the shepherds receiving in the Christmas story.

These men were caring for sheep out in the field and keeping track of their livestock at night. They were minding their own business, literally, when an angel appeared to them out of the blue. Sometimes I wonder if they mistook the angel for another shepherd, perhaps a bandit, or even just a passerby. But it did not take long for the shepherds to figure out that something divine was happening because suddenly there was this presence of God. Luke calls it the "glory of the Lord."

Was the glory of God like the pillar of cloud by day or the pillar of fire by night that led the Israelites through the wilderness? Was this glory of God tangible like the incense that Zechariah burned in the Temple the day he encountered God's messenger? Whatever it was, it terrified the shepherds because the first words out of the angel's mouth were, "Do not be afraid." Now friends, if someone surprised me in the middle of the night, angel or no angel, I would be terrified as well. I do not love surprises. Perhaps the shepherds' fear comes from a watchful eye ready for predators. The angel declared, "Do not be afraid. I bring you good news that will cause great joy for all the people. Today in the town of David a Savior has been born to you; he is the Messiah, the Lord. This will be a sign to you: You will find a baby wrapped in cloths and lying in a manger" (Luke 2:10-12).

God gives these unlikely shepherds a sign: you will discover a baby wrapped in cloths and resting in a manger. Who were these shepherds? They were third-shift workers in charge of watching of sheep in the town of Bethlehem through the night. They had a job to do. Shepherding had its hazards: extreme temperatures, predators to fend off, and looters to keep out of the fold. Although necessary for the job, the shepherds seemed to be considered a first-century nuisance at best. As part of the working class, shepherds had a mixed reputation. When it comes to the socioeconomic ladder, these guys were near the bottom. The shepherds were considered quite unlikely.

> When it comes to the socioeconomic ladder, these guys were near the bottom. The shepherds were considered quite unlikely.

Why would the God of the universe choose shepherds as primary witnesses to the birth of the Savior of the world? Why make this announcement; why give this sign to a strange group of shepherds? Sometimes in our telling of the Christmas story we are tempted to give the shepherds a bad reputation. We place labels on them. I have heard people call them dirty. We shade their character. Could it be that God's choosing of the shepherds pointed to a deeper truth? Somehow, these shepherds further help us understand the character of God.

I had to kneel making my way into the Church of the Nativity in Bethlehem. The doors were lowered in the early 1500s to keep potential looters out and pilgrims from flooding in. And on that particular September day, pilgrims were flooding in by the dozens. Although tourism had begun to pick back up in the Holy Land in the aftermath of the pandemic lockdown, I wasn't expecting that many people. We all seemed to be milling about for the same purpose, to make our way to the Grotto of the Nativity. Our guide hurried us along. He seemed desperate to get us in the line that was forming quickly.

The temperatures were record high outside, and with so many bodies pressed together inside we all started to sweat. We kept inching our way forward. And that inching quickly morphed into pushing and shoving. No one was particularly unkind, but it seemed like a bit of chaos. For anyone who has made the journey to the grotto, there is a mixture of emotions: anticipation and confusion, awe and annoyance.

Sometimes it was hard to imagine the simple and unlikely among the centuries of ornate décor and exquisiteness inside the church. The smells of an ancient building combined with incense and sweat lingered in the air. But soon the heat, the sweat, the pushing, and the slight anger of the crowd grounded my experience. There was something holy in humans rushing to catch a glimpse of the supposed spot of Jesus's birth. We rushed to take a peek at the holy, to touch the divine. Suddenly I felt like we were all longing for something beyond our natural experience.

By the time my mom and I made our way down the narrow stairwell, there was a break in the crowd. I really did not know what I was supposed to do. We had long ago ditched our guide. I people-watched and observed as folks knelt near the grotto touching the fourteen-point star revealing the rock below. Some pilgrims left behind flowers; others were prostrate kissing the ground. I was not prepared with flowers, and a kiss felt way too disingenuous. But I wanted to touch the holy spot.

I watched as persons attempted to kneel, and some struggled, but I knew I could be limber and quick. So, I went for it. I reached out and touched the star. I longed to touch the holy, to have a divine encounter with God. I wanted a sign. Like Jesus at his baptism or even the Mount of Transfiguration. For a moment the heavens would open, and God would declare, "This is my Son, whom I love; with him I am well pleased" (Matthew 3:17). Did that happen? Absolutely not. In fact, I felt a touch of guilt for even touching the star because I did not wait my turn. Self-awareness kept me from lingering too long.

> I longed to touch the holy, to have
> a divine encounter with God.
> I wanted a sign.

Distracted by the hurry of the people around me, I quickly realized that church officials were clearing the space. Preparations were being made for a special ceremony, and they were shooing people out of the grotto. It is difficult not to carry unrealistic expectations into these holy places and spaces. I mean come on, God, if you are going to show up in spectacular ways, why not in the Holy Land?

Our group made our way through the city, meeting families making a living from the olive trees that lined the hillsides. The day was packed full of hurry and by the time we left Bethlehem, I was distracted. I felt oblivious to the walls surrounding the city, the government checkpoints, the politics that encompassed Bethlehem. I was not paying attention to Bethlehem until our tour guide said, "Look to your right and you will see a modern-day shepherd."

To my surprise, the shepherd he was gesturing to was a woman. "A woman?" I thought to myself. It never dawned on me that women could be shepherds. I had questions. "Is this common?" I asked our guide.

An Unlikely Advent

"Of course, there are women who shepherd, Rachel," he answered. "Shepherding is a family affair."

Certainly, I have witnessed a young girl or two cast as shepherds during a Christmas pageant, but to see a woman herding the sheep in Bethlehem caused me to question my assumptions about shepherds. Have I placed the shepherds in a category they do not belong? Have I assumed that these shepherds were marginalized and despised by their communities? It should not surprise us that shepherding was a major theme throughout the whole of the biblical narrative.

Think about the bigger picture with me. King David, arguably the most esteemed king of Israel, was a shepherd. His story is that his leadership training began with his days as a shepherd. He learned to organize, care for, and defend his sheep on the hillsides of Bethlehem. David, the shepherd and later king of Israel wrote, "The LORD is my shepherd, I lack nothing. He makes me lie down in green pastures, he leads me beside quiet waters, he refreshes my soul" (Psalm 23:1-3a).

> God is our shepherd, rather than our king. Imagine the political implications of understanding leadership and power in the hands of unlikely shepherds.

God is our shepherd, rather than our king. Imagine the political implications of understanding leadership and power in the hands of unlikely shepherds. Jesus himself frequently used the parables and metaphors about sheep and shepherds: "I am the good shepherd. The good shepherd lays down his life for the sheep" (John 10:11).

Jesus could be trusted. And not only Jesus and David, but also Moses was the shepherd of God's people. Moses had a divine encounter with God while shepherding. He was out watching over the sheep away from other people. He had isolated himself from his past, attempting to leave Egypt behind. But all of it was merely training for his purpose.

Moses had learned to care for sheep and, like David, shepherding had become a training ground for his leadership. Moses delivered the people out of Egypt and set God's people free. Why did I not see this before? Sometimes I become so hyper-focused on a particular story in Scripture, that I forget the bigger picture. I forget God's plan of healing and restoration for the whole wide world. For years I have missed the forest for the trees and forgotten that God chooses the unlikely, and God selects the shepherd types for God's restorative work. Shepherds are regular everyday people.

Care and humility are folded right into God's choosing of the shepherds. Although the unlikely, these shepherds were getting ready to receive a front row seat to God's salvation. God seemed to be leveling the playing field. Every valley was being exalted and every mountain brought down low. God's choosing of the shepherds was a huge contrast to the likes of Herod the Great, or even the shepherds and the powers of Rome. It is our human tendency to look to the powerful and the privileged, to the bold and the beautiful for answers. But shepherds flip the script.

It is frustrating, because I want to cling to the bold and spectacular parts of the story: the angel choir, the heavenly skies lighting up with bursts of holiday celebrations. I want a sign. But unlikely? I am not too sure about unlikely. Unlikely leaves a bland taste in our mouths. No one really wants to be unlikely, common, or even average. Shepherds. God, really, why did you choose these shepherds? Perhaps God has something to teach those of us always looking for signs.

> **Perhaps God has something to teach those of us always looking for signs.**

Modern-Day Shepherds

There *are* modern-day shepherds in our midst. People who do the hard work, who are willing to take late-night shifts. I wonder if instead of herding sheep they herd people: men and women working late nights and probably not expecting anything spectacular to happen in their ordinary lives. They are bus drivers, hospital transporters, TSA, and taxi drivers.

Do not let me forget the Uber drivers. I cannot imagine all that Uber drivers experience and the stories that they could tell about the habits of humans: what people say, what people do, the messes people bring into their vehicles. Any time of the day or night, an Uber driver receives a message and follows it to the destination. Uber drivers herd people from here to there and everywhere in-between.

A couple of years ago, I was in Orlando speaking at a conference and I needed an Uber to the airport. I was tired, perhaps a little cranky, and ready to be on my way home from a busy weekend. I needed peace.

I was surprised by the speed by which my Uber driver came to pick me up. I waited for only what seemed like seconds and

Renaldo was there. Renaldo was attentive, friendly, and ready to help. He wanted to make sure that I had everything I needed. When I settled into the back seat of his SUV, I noticed that he had fresh bottled water in the cupholders and phone charging cords for any and every phone imaginable. He was ready for anyone or anything.

Renaldo's car was clean, really clean. And for a momma of four who transports kids all the time, I was impressed. Renaldo and I exchanged hellos and I expected that to be the end of our conversation. This is the moment that the Uber ride becomes quiet, either because the driver is not much of a conversationalist, or I am too tired to talk. But not Renaldo. Renaldo made some small talk and was genuinely interested in what brought me to Orlando.

"Rachel," he said in what seemed to be a Latino accent, "what do you do?"

Usually I say something like "I work with people." Telling strangers that I am a preacher leads to a lot of explanation. It can be fun to ask people to guess. They never guess correctly, but it is fun to ask. And did I mention I was tired and wanted some peace? This time I was too tired to beat around the bush with Renaldo. So, I said, "Renaldo, I'm a preacher and I was speaking at a conference." Renaldo's eyes grew wide! He smiled as though I had just made the best announcement ever. Suddenly there was a shift in the conversation.

"Preacher," Renaldo said, "you are an answer to my prayers. You can help me."

Help? Friends, that was not the plan for my trip. I was not looking to help Renaldo. But I was riding in his SUV and Renaldo had my listening ear, whether I liked it or not. Renaldo took that moment to share his heart and his story with me.

Renaldo raised his family in New York City and was devoted to his Roman Catholic faith. And he wanted to talk with me about the Bible reading for the day, but not in English, in Spanish. Lord Jesus, please help me. I know a little Greek, a little German, a little French, but the only Spanish I know I learned on Sesame Street: *uno, dos, tres.* I leaned in and listened hard. And praise God, the words of the Gospel reading were familiar enough for me to recognize the story.

It was the story of Zacchaeus from Luke 19. Renaldo had questions about faith, about life, about what it means to be a generous follower of Jesus. "Why? Why give so much away? Jesus said that salvation has come to Zacchaeus's house. Rachel, what does salvation have to do with money?" We talked at length about generosity and the way that generosity can free us from the hold that money and material belongings have on our hearts.

Then Renaldo said to me, "Rachel, there are a lot of people who don't believe in anything. People are way too rushed to believe. The world needs people who are willing to give of themselves not just receive. I wish they knew there is a great God who can help." Now Renaldo was preaching to me.

Renaldo went on to share with me about his family, which is like many of our families: kids struggling to find their way, portions of the family that are estranged as well as family members needing better employment. He wanted so desperately for these United States of America to be the land of promise that he had envisioned for everyone he knew. As he talked passionately about his family, Renaldo asked me to pray.

My Roman Catholic Uber driver was asking me, the woman preacher, to pray for him and his family. And so, I said, "Renaldo, let's pray now, let's not wait. You keep your eyes on the road and let me pray over you and your family." He drove and I prayed. And by the time I said "Amen" we were at the terminal.

But then something extraordinary happened. Renaldo put the SUV in park and let loose. He began praying over me, as deeply and as passionately as he could. Renaldo prayed for me, prayed for my church, prayed for God to bring us together again the next time I made my way to Orlando. The presence of God filled that SUV as Renaldo's prayer took my breath away. I had tears.

What started out as an ordinary Uber ride became so much more. I was supposed to be sharing God's love with Renaldo and giving my Bible knowledge to him, but this modern-day shepherd was so generously sharing God's love with me. And it was a sign to me. It was God showing up in unlikely places with unlikely people.

> Could it be that we have gotten
> the shepherds all wrong?
> Could it be that we are looking
> in the wrong places for signs?

Could it be that we have gotten the shepherds all wrong? Could it be that we are looking in the wrong places for signs? I should not have been surprised about Renaldo and his relentless sharing of God's good news. The shepherds after their divine encounter could not help but share their experience: "So they hurried off and found Mary and Joseph, and the baby, who was lying in the manger. When they had seen him, they spread the word concerning what had been told them about this child, and all who heard it were amazed at what the shepherds said to them" (Luke 2:16-18).

Much like Renaldo, there was no fear in the shepherds. No regard for what others thought about their position or reputation. These shepherds let loose on anyone who was willing to listen. They told everyone what the angels had said about this child. God had shown up in their ordinary lives. What a sign and what a story. And that is the Bible. The Christmas story is full of the unlikely: an unlikely teenage girl becomes pregnant with the Holy Spirit. God rejected the powerful and those who are seated in palaces and selects a very unlikely place for the birth of God's one and only Son: Bethlehem. The sign was strange. Jesus's birth seems tucked away, nearly hidden from the eyes of anyone who was anyone. No Facebook, no Insta-story, no Buzz Feed or TMZ. Jesus's birth was less dramatic than the birth of John the Baptist. At the very core of this sign was humility. God showed up. This baby king was born in a cave-like stable where animals slept. As a kid who grew up on a farm, I imagine even the animals were wondering, What is going on? Unlikely.

Steady shepherds were in the field just outside of Bethlehem. They remind me of my dad. When I was growing up, my dad worked twelve-hour swing shifts for Dupont. And my dad was not automatically off work on Christmas Day. Many years he had to work the holidays. I remember as a child getting up really, really early before my dad left for work some Christmas mornings. Or as a young kid I had to wait to open gifts until he got home from working all night.

Perhaps your mom or dad was a modern-day shepherd too. Most of the time, Dad seemed tired, quiet, and ready to go to bed. Do not misunderstand what I am saying about my father. Dad was nice and enjoyed what he saw. It was just that sometimes Christmas felt like another ordinary day, just an ordinary workday for my dad. He was a modern-day shepherd. Shepherds in the first century were not necessarily the most popular of folks; some scholars believed first-century shepherds were scorned and not always trusted.[1] And yet they were consistent, faithful, doing what they did every night: protecting the sheep, making a living.

But then they suddenly experienced a divine sign. The heavens were split open and angels showed up. The shepherds had to be scared out of their minds. The Bible says, "They were terrified" (Luke 2:9). I mean if the God of the universe showed up at Dupont or the gas station or in the middle of your third shift, wouldn't you be terrified? God's sign was and is on purpose: the unlikely meets the miraculous and the angel hosts shout: "Glory to God in the highest heaven, and on earth peace to those on whom his favor rests" (Luke 2:14) Right here, right now, on earth! God has an announcement to make, not on Facebook, not breaking news on a global platform. God makes the announcement in a shepherd's field.

> Do you expect a sign of the miraculous in the middle of the night? Do you expect God to show up in your unlikely?

Maybe you feel like a shepherd working third shift at Waffle House or the gas station. Maybe you're an emergency room nurse or a police officer. Maybe—just maybe—you've had a third-shift experience as you get up early for crying children, or your body has forced you to endure the third shift as you struggle to sleep at night. Do you expect a sign of the miraculous in the middle of the night? Do you expect God to show up in your unlikely?

When God Shows Up

Throughout Advent, Christmas Eve, and Christmas Day we will celebrate and then we will go back to our ordinary lives. But here is the thing; sometimes when the singing is all over, when we pack away the Christmas trees, when we have eaten that last Christmas cookie, there is this feeling of emptiness that can seep into our hearts and minds. The family gatherings are over, the presents are unwrapped, the sanctuary no longer decorated, and everything seems duller, less bright. We know that feeling; it can leave us feeling down and nearly depressed. But I believe the experience is good and grounding, because it is in the ordinary and unlikely that God does God's best work.

> God is always present in our lives; it is just that we sometimes need to open ourselves and our schedules to God's presence.

At the night shift at the hospital, God shows up. When we are taxiing our kids from activity to activity, God shows up. When getting dressed for work or school, God shows up. While pouring that thousandth bowl of cereal or in the line at the grocery store, God shows up. God is always present in our lives; it is just that we sometimes need to open ourselves and our schedules to God's presence.

I imagine that many of us come to the Advent and Christmas seasons expecting to feel all the feelings, to experience God's presence, and to be moved by our worship celebrations. The desire to experience God in church is good. God is present when we gather. But the really good news of this holiday is that Jesus is Immanuel, God with us all the time. We get these daily memos, these signs; they come to us in every way, every day. It is not hocus-pocus, but you have to be focused.

How do we focus on God's presence? How do we experience the Christ of Christmas beyond the season? Well, what helps me focus is terribly ordinary. It is prayer. Perhaps to you that sounds like a simple, trite answer. Medical researchers suggest that prayer and meditation are a force that help us focus. We can experience peace in the middle of our holiday anxiety.

Every morning I spend time in prayer on Facebook. I livestream the prayer mostly to keep myself accountable and consistent. I do not filter how I look or even how my children are behaving (or not so behaving) on any given day. I need to show up. Because the anxiety of my daily life creeps into my head and heart and without daily prayer, I feel off balance. And my prayer is not limited to the morning. When I need to recharge, I light a candle on my desk and ask for my body to be open to the movement of the Holy Spirit. I want to step into that flow when it is easy to feel it and when I absolutely do not feel it.

Prayer gives us space to be, space to hear, and space to listen. Here is the not-so-great news: that means we must slow down. Just writing those words makes me cringe a little. I am not good at slowing down, and that's why I so desperately need prayer. Prayer to help me wake up and bear witness to the fact that God is already present in the seemingly unlikely places of my life and yours.

Could it be that in our ordinary, everyday moments that God is longing to give us a sign? God is present and available; God's grace is at our fingertips. It is not that God no longer gives us signs, or that God is asleep. Sometimes we can think that God's just waiting for us to do something so that God can be good. No, God is already good and already present. It's simply our job to align ourselves with God's presence in the world. The signs are all around us.

Unlikely Signs through Unlikely People

Over and over again the Gospel writer of Luke placed a spotlight on the most unlikely of people: Zechariah and Elizabeth, Herod, and yes, even the unlikely shepherds. But Luke does not stop there. There were also the unlikely Anna and Simeon, two persons who gave their days and lives to the worship of God in the Temple. They reduced the pace of their lives. Anna and Simeon were patient enough to wait for a sign, a divine promise. But there was also Zacchaeus, who climbed a tree to catch a glimpse of Jesus. Thumbing through Luke's Gospel, every other chapter brings an unlikely scenario to mind. And it was not just the Gospel; it was also the second volume of Luke in the Book of Acts. Acts was chock-full of unlikely people having God-encounters, unlikely people like Dorcas.

When I was growing up in a small country church, we had a practice of hosting an annual Christmas pageant. There were songs to sing, lines to learn, and roles to be awarded to the most boisterous kids in our children's ministry. Although I was shy as a kid, I had a deep desire to be a star. That particular year, I had my sights on playing the role of Mary. I was old enough, mature enough, and ready (at least I thought so) to stand on the stage representing the very woman who gave birth to Jesus. There was just one problem: my mom was helping direct the pageant that year and she did not play favorites.

My mom had an extra chromosome of fairness and believed that directors' kids should not receive the most important roles. And for whatever reason, this particular Christmas play was full of interesting characters: talking cows and donkeys, the innkeeper and his wife, as well as a few random Bible characters. So, when the roles in the play were announced, not only was I not cast as Mary, but I was horrified when my mom declared I would be playing the role of Dorcas. Dorcas? I would not be cast as any of the famous players encircling the sweet baby Jesus that Christmas morning. Dorcas was certainly more like an adjunct, much-less-glamorous write-in.

Of course, my older brother could not let that go. "Dorcas, yes! Rachel is a Dorcas!" he exclaimed with glee. With a combination of grief and preteen angst, I stormed out of the sanctuary and plopped down on the church steps in a pool of tears. That was when I heard the warm gentle voice of my Sunday school teacher say, "Rachel, I know you are upset, and I know older brothers can sometimes pick on us, but do you even know who Dorcas is?"

"Dorcas isn't a real person!" I shouted through my tears. "Who on earth would ever name their kid Dorcas! I cannot believe my mom is making me be Dorcas. I wanted to be Mary!"

Anyone but Dorcas

That's when my Sunday school teacher opened the Bible to the New Testament Book of Acts chapter 9 and read me this story. Peter had been traveling throughout towns beyond Jerusalem. He stopped near the coast to a place called Lydda. In a neighboring city of Joppa there lived a woman described as a disciple of Jesus named Tabitha, an Aramaic name translated from the Greek name Dorcas. Dorcas was committed to following Jesus in word and deed. She was known for her care for the poor and widows. And when she became sick, the whole community of faith worried. Before long, Dorcas died, and her body was taken to an upper room.

When the followers of Jesus from Joppa heard that Peter was in the neighboring town, they decided to request his presence. "Please come at once!" they urged (Acts 9:38). Peter did. Peter cared enough for the woman who cared so much for others that he left where he was staying immediately. Now, women in the first century were not always valued, and yet Peter valued this woman even to save her life. When Peter arrived at the home, he was led upstairs where the women surrounding Dorcas were mourning. In their grief, they shared with Peter all the clothes that she had made for them when she was alive. Peter had compassion on the whole group and asked them to leave the room. And what did Peter do? He prayed. Luke writes,

> *Turning toward the dead woman, he said, "Tabitha, get up."*
> *She opened her eyes, and seeing Peter she sat up. He took her*
> *by the hand and helped her to her feet. Then he called for the*
> *believers, especially the widows, and presented her to them alive.*

*This became known all over Joppa, and many people believed
in the Lord.*

Acts 9:40-42

Who is this Dorcas? Perhaps we have a few clues: Dorcas
cared for these widows. So much so that they were showing Peter
the clothes she made for them. And when I say clothes she made,
I am not talking about garments that they kept in the closets at
home. These are first-century widows with a limited wardrobe.
We are literally talking about what they are wearing. There was
no government assistance in the first century. There was only the
church. Men and women who stepped up to care for the most
vulnerable in their congregations. And this was Dorcas's claim to
fame. She was an amazing servant, leader, movement-maker, and
unlikely person in God's unfolding story.

> And this was Dorcas's claim
> to fame. She was an amazing
> servant, leader, movement-maker,
> and unlikely person in God's
> unfolding story.

Suddenly it is not the most famous, it is not the bold and the
beautiful, it is not the coolest and most attractive; but rather we see
heaven come to earth when faithful people step up to play center
stage in the story of God's kingdom. Dorcas was faithful, not
famous. Could it be that God is asking you and me to be more like
the shepherds and Dorcas? They are the ones providing clothing
for vulnerable communities, the people preparing meals in food

deserts, and the group leaders sharing their lives with strangers in prisons. People who are looking to what is in their hands and using it for the glory of God, not the glory of themselves. They are unlikely people.

In culture where many strive to be noticed on social media, the Dorcases of the world do not try to be someone else. Dorcas was not offered the role of Mary, she did not have Peter's authority, and yet she did not despise the gifts that God gave her. Most of the time we are not offered the role and function that we would prefer in life. And yet Dorcas's story was the story that God wanted to tell so that you and I might recognize that no matter how seemingly insignificant or obscure our gifts, skills, and abilities, whatever we have in our hands God uses to have a major impact in the lives of the people around us. God does God's best through the unlikely people.

And so I played Dorcas in the Christmas pageant. She served as a narrator of sorts. Although Mary never uttered a single word in this play, Dorcas carried the storyline. Dorcas proclaimed that God used the most unlikely people (and animals) in telling of Jesus's birth, talking cows and all. Perhaps my mom realized what she was doing all along, helping her daughter experience God's bigger picture, God's plan for her unlikely story. Mom knew I couldn't remain quiet for an entire Christmas play.

Your Unlikely Story

God is already on the move in our story, showing up in our dark nights and ordinary days. It is up to us to step into the flow of God's presence and open our eyes to the unlikely. God shows up in the day-to-day. God shows up when we are tired, when we are working the late-night shift, and when we don't feel like talking to the Uber driver. God shows up when we do not think we have the energy to be a blessing in someone else's life.

Two thousand years ago, God showed up on a hillside and appeared to a group of ordinary shepherds, giving them a sign that would change the whole wide world. And God shows up in our lives to remind us, "For to us a child is born, to us a son is given, and the government will be on his shoulders. And he will be called Wonderful Counselor, Mighty God, Everlasting Father, Prince of Peace" (Isaiah 9:6).

Perhaps you feel like you could not see the star if your life depended on it. You are an unlikely person with an unlikely job with a regular house in an ordinary neighborhood. You have allowed yourself to be counted out or relegated to the sidelines of God's kingdom. You have clung tighter to Herod's Judea and the emperor's Rome, a culture of comparison and competition, rather than the God who gives dream-like guidance to the magi and a sign to unlikely shepherds. You still are just looking for a sign.

> God's love came from heaven
> in a form so we could see,
> experience, and understand the
> divine right in front of us.

In the hurry and the chaos of our every day, we can forget that God's presence and power are available to us if we would just open our eyes and our schedules to God's presence. God's invitation for us today remains the same: God is here and God is present. The Word, Jesus, became flesh and blood as a vulnerable infant child and moved into our neighborhood. God's love came from heaven in a form so we could see, experience, and understand the divine right in front of us.

Jesus is Immanuel, God with us, in order that you and I could have life, right here, right now on earth as it is in heaven. God flipped the script at Advent and Christmas so that we could receive the peace and presence of Christ. And I wonder, have you ever asked for Christ's peace? Have you ever asked God to rewrite your unlikely story?

For a moment I want to invite you to imagine yourself just doing what you do: your everyday life. Maybe you are at work teaching kids how to read, or you have the late-night shift at the hospital, or you are in boardrooms. Some of you work at home, and still others are busier in so-called retirement than you have ever been before. It is just day-to-day survival until one day you experience a glimpse of the divine. Suddenly you recognize Christ's unlikely presence. Maybe it is not big and bold as an angelic appearance, but your awareness makes you shiver. You hear a voice: *Do not be afraid. I am here, I am present. Come and see.*

God invites you to come and see this child wrapped in cloth and lying in a manger. It was terribly ordinary. The manger was a sign, a space for animals to be fed. The sign was not a billboard. The sign was not the glory of God, but rather the sign was simple, a feeding trough for livestock. This manger reminds us that God chose the most unlikely of places and people to share God's unfolding story. God extends the invitation, again and again. God invites us in until our eyes and ears are open. God's invitation is an invitation into being and not to doing this Advent season. Just rest in God's presence for a moment. Take a big deep breath.

Have you ever given yourself permission to slow down with Jesus? God gave the shepherds permission to leave the field and sit at the manger. You have permission to leave your desk, to set the laundry aside, to close your laptop, and to sit at the manger with Jesus. You can witness this sign just like the angels proclaimed, "You will find a baby wrapped in cloths and lying in a manger" (Luke 2:12). In the hustle and bustle of the holiday season we can forget that Jesus is the Prince of Peace, not the prince of busyness, not the leader of hurry, but rather the one who offers us peace and rest.

> **You have permission to leave your desk, to set the laundry aside, to close your laptop, and to sit at the manger with Jesus.**

Perhaps it is fitting to finish our time together receiving Christ's peace and presence. I invite you to sit in a comfortable position, if you are able to lay your hands on your lap, palms facing up as sign that you are ready to receive. Take a deep breath and let me pray over you.

God of the unlikely, you have come from heaven to earth to create the opportunity for us to encounter you every single day. There are signs all around us. In the middle of our hurried, anxious lives, give us real rest and fill us with your peace. Help us to receive your presence and to share it with everyone we encounter. Let us live into our unlikely purpose. Amen.

EPILOGUE

I am a reluctant learner, particularly when it comes to giving God the opportunity to invade my daily schedule. I have things to do and people to see. Most of the time I have a clear picture of the days and weeks ahead. And certainly, during the Advent season, I am not expecting the unlikely to happen. But leave it to God to continue to challenge me to experience God in the most unlikely of places.

My husband, Jon, and I were leaving the ophthalmologist's office from a checkup following our daughter Sarah's second eye surgery. Our youngest's Marfan syndrome had rendered her legally blind, and she needed her lenses removed from both eyes for a shot at future eyesight. It was December and we were focused on caring for our daughter. It was not lost on me that if the surgery was successful, what Sarah would experience would be a miracle of sorts. When your child experiences a miracle during Advent, it just makes a momma feel so much closer to the Nativity story.

The doctor had suggested a few items for Sarah's care at home, so Jon and I stopped at the grocery store to pick them up. We were in a hurry to get Sarah home, so I left Sarah and Jon in the car as I jogged into the grocery store. I had never been to this particular store and so the layout was unfamiliar. I began frantically searching for the items that I needed. Sunglasses: check. Pain meds: check. Bubble gum: check.

As I gathered up my items and headed to check out, I noticed a woman in the self-checkout who did not seem like she was feeling well. "No thank you," I said out loud to myself. I veered away from self-checkout to take my chances with a cashier. But the woman soon cried out, "Help me, somebody, help me!"

I looked to the sky and said, "Not today, Lord! I have done my good deeds for the day! Not today!" But when I turned around, I saw the young woman being helped by a frail man who could barely stand on his own feet. So, I rushed to her side to keep her from falling. She had been sick that day with a stomach virus she informed me and felt as if she was going to pass out. A grocery store employee called for an ambulance and with desperation in her eyes she begged me, "Do not leave me, please!"

I reassured that I would not leave. I quickly was able to gather information that she worked for a preschool housed in a local church just down the street. And with her cell phone at my disposal, I was able to talk to her director as well as her husband. The employee brought her a seat, and as soon as she was sitting, she leaned against me, holding on for dear life. "Sweet Jesus," I prayed, "Do not let me get sick!" It was the third week in Advent, and Christmas was a little over a week away. I did not have this scheduled for my day.

Within minutes, the woman's fellow preschool teachers arrived to help. Together we were able to secure the groceries she needed. The teachers were followed by medical professionals. I knew my family would be wondering what on earth happened to my quick trip to the grocery store, but I waited until the woman was firmly in the hands of the EMTs to gather my items and pay for them at checkout.

My heart was racing, and before she was wheeled away, I reassured her that I would be praying for her to be well. I could not help but think of Mary as this young woman. So often we believe that the Nativity scene is clean and pristine, but it is not lost on me that Mary would have called out for help in the silence of the night of Jesus's birth. Is a stable in Bethlehem so different from the self-checkout line? God is with us in the very mess that we call human existence. There is something so profoundly grounding about human suffering. When we are vulnerable with one other it is as if we are given a glimpse of God. In these moments of helpless desperation, I am torn between my calendar and the holy encounter. I am teetering between the busy and the broken. God centers me somewhere between the urgent and the unlikely. I could not help but look up at the sky this time and smirk, "Funny, God, real funny," as I soon would be preaching about unlikely encounters.

As I stood up, I began looking for a restroom. I wanted to gather my thoughts and wash my hands. By the time I had finished washing, I ran into one of the preschool teachers who reassured me that the woman was going to be okay. The medics were merely taking the woman to the hospital for observation. "Most likely dehydration," she explained.

"Thank you," I said as I headed to the door.

I know I can be an unlikely disciple of Jesus. With a calendar stacked to the edges, one would think I had no time for an unlikely encounter. But that is the thing about God. God works in the unlikely spaces of our lives. God works whether we are too busy or not. God must consider grocery stores holy ground, because that was not the first and will not be the last time that I have had a divine encounter with God in a grocery store.

We serve an unlikely God who empowered Zechariah and Elizabeth to dream forward, a God who chose the unlikely Herod as villain in our Advent story, a God who extended the edges of God's table to include the likes of the magi, and a God who showed up in the regular lives of unlikely shepherds to announce the birth of Jesus. You and I are a part of God's unlikely story. God empowers us and deploys us to experience God's unlikely every single day. Open yourself up to unlikely adventures, and together we will experience God in ways we could not even ask or imagine.

ACKNOWLEDGMENTS

I want to express my deep gratitude to Maria Mayo, Susan Salley, and the entire team at Abingdon Press. I am grateful for the opportunity to share this Advent journey with the wider church. Maria, I praise God for your patience with me and my constant need to talk it out.

To the leadership of New Albany United Methodist Church, thank you for giving me space to create and do what I love. And to my worship design team, Jean Schafer, Lyndsey Casey, Mike Pratt, and Jenn Klima, you all make me better. As always, here is a shout out to my message coach Kim Miller who brings out the best in me and everyone she works with.

Thank you to my husband, Jon Billups, and my kiddos, Addie, Topher, David, and Sarah. I love our life and our family!

And finally, to my momma, Linda Fast, thank you for having the courage to travel with me to the Holy Land. It's turning out to be a trip of a lifetime.

NOTES

Chapter 2: Playing the Villain

1   Yigael Yadin et al., "Masada" in *The New Interpreters Dictionary of the Bible* (Nashville: Abingdon Press, 2009), 828.

2   "Masada," *The New Interpreters Dictionary of the Bible*, 828.

3   Carl Rasmussen, *Atlas of the Bible*, rev. ed. (Grand Rapids: Zondervan, 2010), 199.

4   Laura A. Bischoff, "Nearly 1 in 3 Go Back to Ohio Prisons," *Columbus Dispatch*, May 28, 2021, https://www.dispatch .com/story/news/2021/05/28/ohio-sees-steady-climb-prison -recidivism-rate/5143605001/.

Chapter 3: A Curious People

1   R.V.G. Tasker, *The Gospel According to St. Matthew: An Introduction and Commentary* in Tyndale New Testament Commentaries (Grand Rapids, Eerdmans, 1962), 41.

2   Jerome Murphy-O'Connor, "Bethlehem" in *The New Interpreters Dictionary of the Bible*, 443.

3   Bruce J. Malina, "Magi" in *The New Interpreter's Dictionary of the Bible*, 766.

4   M. Eugene Boring, "Matthew" in *The New Interpreter's Bible Commentary*, vol. 7 (Nashville: Abingdon Press, 2015), 77.

Notes

Chapter 4: When God Shows Up

1   R. Alan Culpepper, "The Gospel of Luke" in the *The New Interpreter's Bible Commentary*, vol. 8 (Nashville: Abingdon Press, 2015), 49.

Watch videos
based on
*An Unlikely Advent:
Extraordinary People
of the Christmas Story*
with Rachel Billups
through Amplify Media.

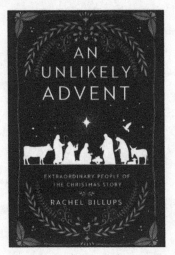

Amplify Media is a multimedia platform that delivers high quality, searchable content with an emphasis on Wesleyan perspectives for churchwide, group, or individual use on any device at any time. In a world of sometimes overwhelming choices, Amplify gives church leaders and congregants media capabilities that are contemporary, relevant, effective and, most importantly, affordable and sustainable.

With *Amplify Media* church leaders can:

+ Provide a reliable source of Christian content through a Wesleyan lens for teaching, training, and inspiration in a customizable library
+ Deliver their own preaching and worship content in a way the congregation knows and appreciates
+ Build the church's capacity to innovate with engaging content and accessible technology
+ Equip the congregation to better understand the Bible and its application
+ Deepen discipleship beyond the church walls

**Ask your group leader or pastor about Amplify Media
and sign up today at www.AmplifyMedia.com.**